Reviews of the first edition

'In short, a clearly-written, sometimes compelling introduction to the theory and practice of textual analysis of British newspapers.'
Language Today

'A well thought out route map which points students towards a deeper understanding of the way that text can be transformed, manipulated, distorted, re-fashioned in written, oral and electronic means.'
Speaking English

'This is language analysis at its best. Safe in the hands of an expert, the reader begins to understand not only the what of newspaper language but also the how and the why.'
Jennifer Greatrex, Examiner, A Level English Language

'An invaluable textbook for students and teachers in English language courses as well as in media and cultural studies.'
Joanna Thornborrow, University of Cardiff

The Language of Newspapers explores the ways in which the press portrays current events. From the ideological bias of the press, to the role of headlines in newspaper articles and ways in which newspapers relate to their audience, the book provides a comprehensive analysis of newspaper language.

The second edition has been substantially rewritten and includes a range of new texts. Features include:

- recent newspaper articles on a range of subjects, including the Blairs, Jeffrey Archer, the British journalist captured for suspected spying in Afghanistan, Mary Bell, and James Bulger's killers
- a new introduction, taking account of recent developments in the media
- new activities to support student-directed study
- a 'further resources' section with details of on-line newspapers and urls to visit

Danuta Reah is co-author of *Working with Texts* and a freelance writer and teacher.

The Intertext series

◎ **Why does the phrase 'spinning a yarn' refer both to using language and making cloth?**

◎ **What might a piece of literary writing have in common with an advert or a note from the milkman?**

◎ **What aspects of language are important to understand when analysing texts?**

The Routledge INTERTEXT series aims to develop reader's understanding of how texts work. It does this by showing some of the designs and patterns in the language from which they are made, by placing texts within the context in which they occur, and by exploring relationships between them.

The series consists of a foundation text, *Working with Texts: A core introduction to language analysis*, which looks at language aspects essential for the analysis of texts, and a range of satellite titles. These apply aspects of language to a particular topic area in more detail. They complement the core text and can also be used alone, providing the user has the foundation skills furnished by the core text.

Benefits of using this series:

◎ **Multi-disciplinary** – provides a foundation for the analysis of texts, supporting students who want to achieve a detailed focus on language.

◎ **Accessible** – no previous knowledge of language analysis is assumed, just an interest in language use.

◎ **Student-friendly** – contains activities relating to texts studied, commentaries after activities, highlighted key terms, suggestions for further reading and an index of terms.

◎ **Interactive** – offers a range of task-based activities both for class use and self study.

◎ **Tried and tested** – written by a team of respected teachers and practitioners whose ideas and activities have been trialled independently.

The series editors:

Adrian Beard is Head of English at Gosforth High School, Newcastle upon Tyne, and a chief examiner for A-Level English Literature. He has written and lectured extensively on the subjects of literature and language. His publications include *Texts and Contexts* (Routledge).

Angela Goddard is Senior Lecturer in Language at the Centre for Human Communication, Manchester Metropolitan University, and was Chief Moderator for English Language A-Level Project Research at the Northern Examination and Assessment Board (NEAB), 1983–1995. She is now chair of examiners of A-Level English Language. Her publications include *Researching Language* (second edn, Heinemann, 2000).

Core textbook:

Working with Texts: A core introduction to language analysis (second edn, 2001) Ronald Carter, Angela Goddard, Danuta Reah, Keith Sanger and Maggie Bowring

Satellite titles:

Language and Gender
Angela Goddard and Lindsey Meân Patterson

The Language of Advertising: Written texts, second edition, 2002
Angela Goddard

The Language of Conversation
Francesca Pridham

The Language of Drama
Keith Sanger

The Language of Fiction
Keith Sanger

The Language of Humour
Alison Ross

The Language of ICT: Information and Communication Technology
Tim Shortis

The Language of Magazines
Linda McLoughlin

The Language of Newspapers, second edition, 2002
Danuta Reah

The Language of Poetry
John McRae

The Language of Politics
Adrian Beard

The Language of Speech and Writing
Sandra Cornbleet and Ronald Carter

The Language of Sport
Adrian Beard

The Language of Television
Jill Marshall and Angela Werndly

The Language of Newspapers

Second Edition

 Danuta Reah

Routledge
Taylor & Francis Group

LONDON AND NEW YORK

First published 1998
by Routledge
11 New Fetter Lane, London EC4P 4EE

Simultaneously published in the USA and Canada
by Routledge
29 West 35th Street, New York, NY 10001

Second edition first published 2002

Reprinted 2003, 2004

Routledge is an imprint of the Taylor & Francis Group

© 1998, 2002 Danuta Reah

Typeset in Stone Sans/Stone Serif by RefineCatch Limited, Bungay, Suffolk
Printed and bound in Great Britain by TJ International Ltd, Padstow, Cornwall

British Library Cataloguing in Publication Data
A catalogue record for this book is available from the British Library

Library of Congress Cataloging in Publication Data
A catalog record for this book has been requested

ISBN 0–415–27804–X (Hbk)
ISBN 0–415–27805–8 (Pbk)

contents

acknowledgements

Thank you to everyone who helped me with this book, especially Ken Reah, Alison Ross and Keith Sanger for reading and commenting on the drafts.

Thank you especially to Angela Goddard and Ron Carter for their invaluable editorial support and advice.

Finally, many thanks to the staff of the *Sheffield Star* for allowing me to visit their news room and answering my questions.

Daily Telegraph

'Diana's fingers do the talking', August 29, 1996; 'Blair will quit so Cherie can become a judge', October 1, 2001; '80 migrants try to enter tunnel site', September 1, 2001. All reproduced by permission of *The Telegraph*.

Sun

'I had a nail in me 'ead for 22 years!', January 6, 1997; 'GOTCHA', May 4, 1982; 'Hula Meanie Spurns Sun Readers on Loot', September 9, 1996; 'Salute from the Poms', January 20, 1988; 'Free', November 11, 1997; 'Luxury Life of Bulger Killers', January 9, 2001; 'Archer's Iron Lady', August 10, 2001. All © News International Newspapers Ltd.

Daily Mirror

'Queen snubs 102,625 Readers', July 30, 1996. Reproduced by permission of the *Daily Mirror*.

Daily Mail

'Four-Letter TV Poem Fury', October 12, 1987, 'What a liberty', October 28, 1996; 'The storming of the chunnel', September 3, 2001; 'Spy talk raises fears for the captive mothers', October 1, 2001; 'The Manipulator', April 30, 1998. All © the *Daily Mail*, reproduced by permission of Atlantic Syndication.

Daily Express

'Bell can run but can't hide', April 30, 1998; 'The heat of the night', June 26, 2001; 'Stewardess scoops £135,000', September 3, 2001. All reproduced by permission of the *Daily Express*.

Mail on Sunday

'The eyes have it', September 3, 2001. Reproduced by permission of the *Mail on Sunday*.

Introduction

Who wants yesterday's papers? Yesterday's newspaper is a useful metaphor for something that has lost its value. Yesterday's news isn't news at all. Old newspapers are used for wrapping chips, for wrapping rubbish, for making papier-mâché, for recycling and for throwing away.

This book is all about yesterday's papers, if only because any newspaper written about in this book will be yesterday's paper (or last year's paper) by the time this book is in print.

But it is also about yesterday's papers because they are important. They provide a series of snapshots of our life and our culture, often from a very specific viewpoint. This book is written to look at the way these texts present, and to a certain extent create or at least influence, aspects of our culture and society.

WHAT IS A NEWSPAPER?

The answer to this question seems at first to be so obvious that the question is hardly worth asking. However, it is a serious question, and one that must be addressed if the language of newspapers is to be looked at in any meaningful way.

For the purposes of this book, newspapers will be divided into three kinds: the broadsheet newspapers, that is, the *Telegraph*, the *Independent*, *The Times* and the *Guardian*; the middle-range tabloids, that is, the *Express* and the *Daily Mail*; and the tabloids, that is, the *Sun*, the *Mirror*, the *Star* (this classification is taken from Tunstall, 1996). There are obviously other newspapers that don't fit into this model, for example, local newspapers and newspapers of particular political groups such as the *Socialist Worker*. However, this book will look at the national British press.[1]

The term *newspaper* suggests that the content of a newspaper will be primarily devoted to the news of the day, and some analysis and comment on this news. Newspapers, however, contain a range of items; news, comment and analysis, advertising, entertainment. In fact, the larger part of a newspaper will be devoted to items other than news, for example, TV listings and advertising. A percentage of the news stories will relate to the activities of celebrities, film and TV stars (particularly soap stars), and the activities of the royal family. Is this news?

Activity

Look at the content of one tabloid and one broadsheet newspaper. classify the contents under the following headings (roughly, by number of pages or fractions of pages): news, sport and entertainment, advertising.

Now classify the news under the following headings: home news (i.e., stories about Britain or British people), overseas news.

Classify the home news into: stories about current events, political stories, stories about royalty, stories about other celebrities, other.

Commentary

An editor of the *New York Times* once said that about 60 per cent of the content of his newspaper was advertising. The papers you have looked at may not contain such a high percentage, but it is highly unlikely that the highest percentage of the paper is devoted to news coverage.

A similar analysis carried out on the *Sun* and the *Guardian* of Thursday, 6 September 2001 gave the following figures: (this analysis excludes magazines and pull-out sections, so the *Guardian*'s tabloid magazine is excluded, as is the *Sun*'s television guide.)

Paper	Sun	Guardian
No. of pages	60	34
Pages of news	13.5 (28%)	14 (41%)
Pages of advertising	17 (35%)	8 (24%)
Sport and entertainment	14 (29%)	6 (18%)

An analysis of this kind clearly demonstrates that the major content of a newspaper is not its news reporting. The above analysis clearly shows that news stories are the greatest single item in the *Guardian*, but advertising is the greater element in the tabloid. This may be because the *Guardian* has a tabloid section that has not been included in this analysis. This section contains no news coverage, and if the advertising content of the tabloid had been included, then the percentage of advertising in the *Guardian* might have been higher. The main point is, however, that in both papers, sport, entertainment and advertising occupy a greater number of pages than does news, and the percentage of page space in both cases demonstrates the importance of advertising content to both papers.

A further point that you might have noticed is the extent to which stories about individuals – whether they are celebrities or not – dominate the news, rather than stories about issues. The section on representation of groups (Unit 4) will look at stories about, for example, the gay community that focus exclusively on individuals and the so-called scandal element, rather than looking at the more general problems and processes that these stories represent.

Newspapers are also artefacts of the commercial and political world. For example, before the break-up of the USSR, the pronouncements of the state newspaper *Pravda* were treated with scepticism by Western commentators, as *Pravda* was seen as the mouthpiece of the ruling Communist Party. It was assumed that even if the editor of *Pravda* wanted to oppose the party ideology he would not be allowed to.

The Western democracies, on the other hand, are seen as having a 'free press'. The freedom of the press is a matter of ideological importance, and one that is enshrined, for example, in the US Constitution. This book is concerned with the British press, and examples and analyses will be taken from British newspapers. The British press, too, is seen as free, and though press freedom is not enshrined in a written constitution (the UK doesn't have one), it is a 'given' of our culture – something that we pride ourselves on, but perhaps don't examine too closely.

However, there are certain points that need to be taken into consideration here, before it is possible to accept (or reject) this view of the British press as 'free', and decide exactly what we mean when we talk about press freedom. What is news? Who owns the press? Who pays for newspapers? Should newspapers be politically or ideologically impartial?

WHAT IS NEWS?

News is a late Middle English word that means 'tidings, new information of recent events'. Even if we accept this definition as a useful description of what a newspaper delivers, this definition has to be narrowed, as any happening anywhere in the world could be seen as a recent event – SID SMITH EATS CHOCOLATE BAR – EXCLUSIVE. A more useful definition might be 'information about recent events that are of interest to a sufficiently large group, or that may affect the lives of a sufficiently large group'. This definition allows for the difference between local and national newspapers, and for the differences between newspapers of different countries or cultural groups.

However, this definition is still not satisfactory. As was noted above, everything that happens anywhere in the world is a *recent event*, so someone, somewhere has to decide which, of all the events that have happened over the last 24 hours, are to be included in a specific newspaper, and which are to be excluded. Newspapers can't include everything. These decisions are generally seen as editorial decisions. If an editor excludes an item because he or she thinks that the readership of the newspaper will not be interested in, or do not need, that information, that may be seen as legitimate editorial control. It does mean, though, that these decisions are being made on behalf of the reader. The reader will not be able to comment on that decision, because the reader will probably not be aware that the omitted item of information exists.

The selection of items to put on the news pages may also affect the way in which the reader is presented with the world. For example, a few years ago, newspaper readers were presented with large numbers of stories about attacks by dogs on adults and children. Certain breeds of dog were demonised. Rottweilers became 'devil dogs', and pit bull terriers were given the status of man-eating tigers. This spate of stories may actually have been the prime mover behind changes in legislation that were rather unwisely rushed through Parliament to restrict the ownership and handling of certain breeds. This legislation was revised in 1997 as largely unworkable. Dogs still attack people, and probably always have, but this no longer makes front page stories.

Decisions may be made to exclude information because it is felt necessary to conceal that information from the readership, or to include information that is seen as in some way beneficial to groups other than the readership – the advertisers, the owners of the paper, the political party the owners of the paper support. Again, the readers have little or no control over what is or is not being presented, as they may not have access to other sources of information against which to judge the content of a newspaper.

People who attend public demonstrations often complain afterwards either that a very well-attended demonstration was ignored by the media and therefore, in the eyes of the majority of the population who did not attend, did not happen, or that it was trivialised by the media's focusing on one aspect – an incident of unruly behaviour, for example, or the dress of a celebrity who attended the event. People who have been involved in newsworthy events that have been ignored or misrepresented by the newspapers often find themselves wondering what else may be excluded from coverage, or presented in a misleading way, but this may not be an issue that the majority of readers are particularly aware of.

DO NEWSPAPERS CONTAIN NEWS?

One reason for this is that newspapers are not read entirely for their informative content. Newspapers contain more than just the news of the day, but even the news is presented in a particular way. We talk about 'news stories'. Other texts that deliver information are not referred to as 'stories'. We don't talk about 'report stories' or 'lecture stories' or 'textbook stories'. A story is an 'account of imaginary or past events, narrative tale, anecdote . . . *colloquial* fib'. Why are news stories referred to in a way that gives them the status of fictional accounts? The definition 'account of past events' may to some extent relate to a factual account, but carries the implication of interpretation, elaboration, the creation of a narrative.

Activity

The four following texts are the opening paragraphs of a popular novel, a broadsheet newspaper report, a tabloid newspaper report, an academic paper. Three of the texts (the academic paper and the newspapers) could be seen as texts designed to deliver information; the novel is designed to deliver narrative.

Can you say which text belongs to which genre?

What similarities and differences exist between these texts? You might want to consider overall length of text, sentence length, vocabulary, content, devices used to gain/maintain audience interest.

Text 1: Power Failure

When the power went I was finishing a ten-page report. My office turned black; the computer groaned to a halt. Helpless, I watched the words fade to a ghostly outline that glowed on the screen before vanishing, like the mocking grin of the Cheshire cat.

Text 2: Monarchy Doomed, Say Half of Britons

Six years ago it was unthinkable. Three divorces, an ongoing debate about the royal finances, and one toe-sucking incident later it is reality – more than half of the Queen's subjects believe the royal family is doomed.

Text 3: I had a nail in me 'ead for 22 years!

Dad Robin Hanshaw walked around for 22 years without realising he had a NAIL embedded in his head.

Text 4: A Comparison of Oral and Written Code Elaboration

The Bernstein initiated model of verbal code elaboration and code restriction is well established in sociolinguistic research literature. Studies emanating from England, the United States, and Australia have tended to support the Bernstein thesis of social class differences in language utilisation especially in manipulating the syntactic and semantic components of language which facilitate precision, flexibility and complexity in verbal encoding. Such differences have been noted in both oral and written communication. However, there has been little interest shown to date in comparing elaborated or restricted codes in oral and written language samples for the same subjects, whether of middle or working class origin.

Commentary

Text 1 is from the novel *Tunnel Vision* by Sara Paretsky. Texts 2 and 3 are from the *Guardian* and the *Sun* respectively, 6 January 1997. Text 4 is from an academic paper: M.E. Poole and T.W. Field, in *Language and Speech*, vol. 19.

The overall length of the texts varies considerably, though they are each the first paragraph of the text from which they have been taken. By far the longest, twice as long as any of the other texts, is the extract from the academic paper. The novel and the broadsheet texts are very close: 46 words and 43 words. The shortest text, from the tabloid article, is 28 words long. The number of sentences is different in each case, but the average sentence length in the novel and the two newspapers is very close – 15, 18 and 18.

The word choices of the texts show a similar pattern. Texts 1, 2 and 3 all use words from everyday vocabulary. There are no words that are from specialist fields, and no words that would send the majority of the population to the dictionary. The longest word in any of these three texts is three syllables long. Text 4, on the other hand, uses a number of specialist words and phrases, 'verbal code elaboration', 'sociolinguistics', and a high number of formal, Latinate words. Several words are as many as five syllables long.

The contents of the first three texts also have some similarities. Each text introduces the reader to a character or characters, and gives some information about events and circumstances. Text 4, on the other hand, is very impersonal, and outlines an area of linguistic theory.

The newspaper texts and the novel all seem constructed to arouse and hold the interest of the reader. Paretsky's novel opens with a subordinate clause 'When the power failed . . .' that immediately arouses the reader's curiosity: what happened?

The *Guardian* opens its article with the sentence 'Six years ago it was unthinkable'. The pronoun 'it' has no reference yet. Again, the reader's curiosity is appealed to: what was unthinkable?

The *Sun* uses a different device to interest readers. It presents them with an incredible fact, a device often used by novelists (for example, Kafka opens his short story 'Metamorphosis' with the line 'As Gregor Samsa awoke one morning from uneasy dreams he found himself transformed in his bed into a gigantic insect'). The first three texts also use a range of language devices to make the texts attractive to the reader. There is use of metaphor in texts 1 and 2 ('turned black', 'a ghostly outline', 'like the mocking grin'; 'doomed'), text 3 uses the speaking voice of its main character, as does text 1. None of these devices is found in text 4.

It isn't just that these texts relate to completely different topics. Text 1 is about computer failure, text 2 about the future of the British monarchy, text 3 about an unusual medical situation and text 4 about the way people use language. Any of these topics could have been approached in a different way. Texts 1, 2 and 3 adopt a similar, narrative stance (people and circumstances) which text 4 does not use. Why is it that newspaper texts appear to be closer to texts whose function it is to tell stories than texts whose function it is to deliver information?

Newspapers, therefore, do contain news, in line with the definition given above, but there is some reason to believe that this news may be presented in the form of a story, rather than as information. This point will be looked at again in Unit 6.

WHO OWNS THE PRESS?

An important factor in the existence of a free press is ownership. The owner of a newspaper has the power to influence the content of the paper, its political stance and its editorial perspective. There has probably never been a time when a newspaper owner did not influence in some way what appeared in that paper. A diverse range and a large number of newspaper owners seems to be an important factor in ensuring that as wide a range of views and interests is represented in the press. The pattern in late twentieth-century Britain has been of newspapers coming into the ownership of smaller numbers of competing groups. In 1965, there were 11 companies owning newspapers, and 19 national titles (including 7 Sunday papers). By 1995, 7 companies owned newspapers, and the number of titles had increased to 21 (including 8 Sunday papers).

The situation is even more complex in 2001. Legislation restricting cross-media ownership, that is, any company having a significant stake in several different media organisations, is being reviewed, under pressure from massive global organisations such as Murdoch's News Corporation which publishes four national newspapers that had, in May 2000, 20% of the market.

The *Independent*, that had been launched on the strength of its 'independence' was taken over by the massive Mirror Group Newspapers, which later became Trinity Mirror via another merger. The *Independent* was then sold, as a loss making title, and is now owned by Independent News and Media.

This concentration of newspapers in fewer hands, and in the hands of larger, more diverse organisations, clearly has implications for press freedom.

WHO PAYS FOR NEWSPAPERS?

Newspapers in the West exist within a free market system. If they are not successful commercially they will fail. Competition is seen to operate to ensure a high-quality product. If, the argument runs, the newspaper is of a poor quality, then people will not buy it. The free-market operates on one major premise: profit. To this end, newspapers do not only contain news, they also contain comment, advertising, entertainment. Advertising is a vital source of revenue for all newspapers. Sales and circulation figures are also vital to a newspaper's survival. If these figures are low, then advertisers will not want to pay for space in the newspapers. If the readers of a particular newspaper want to be entertained, want information about celebrities and soap-opera characters, and don't want their received ideas challenged, then editors will give them what they want. Mass-circulation newspapers must cater to the requirements of the mass-market, and in this way, the operation of market forces is likely to work against provision for minority interests, or the development of new areas of interest.

Look back to the analysis you did on p. 2. A brief survey of this kind will quickly establish that newspapers do not primarily concern themselves with news, and the news that they do include is fairly circumscribed as to topic area. Broadsheet newspapers contain slightly more news overall than tabloids, and a lot more overseas news, but the bulk of the content in both cases is devoted to other things.

This is not a problem as such, but it does indicate that even newspapers operating within a free market system are not necessarily going to give a free account of the news of the day.

More worrying, though, is the influence of the advertisers and the owners. Newspapers that attract a lot of advertising can sell their product at a lower price and afford a whole range of devices to make their product attractive to the potential reader. If an advertiser has a luxury product, particularly a luxury food product, to sell, does that advertiser want the audience disturbed by reports of poverty and famine? If a major company has been polluting the environment and supporting state terrorism in a developing country, is that company going to give its lucrative advertising contracts to publications that report these events? Is a paper whose editorial policy is to criticise the capitalist and free market system going to attract any advertising at all? As has already been discussed, newspaper owners are often large corporations with a wide range of commercial and political interests. Will such an owner allow stories that are hostile to his/her commercial or political interests to appear in the paper?

The reader of newspapers, then, is not entirely the recipient of *new information on recent events*. He or she is the recipient of selected information on recent events, and this information may well be presented with an ideological 'spin' that makes it very difficult for the reader to make an independent decision on what his/her actual viewpoint of these events actually is.

SHOULD NEWSPAPERS BE IMPARTIAL?

A further important issue relates to the way news is presented. The analysis carried out on pp. 5–6 above demonstrates that newspapers present facts in a way that is designed to arouse the reader's interest and curiosity. It is also possible to present facts in a way that will influence the reader's view of them. This point will be an important focus of this book, but a brief look here at the political bias that appears to exist currently in the press, and the problems presented by press ownership, will give an important context to the problem of the way newspapers present information to their readers.

Before 1970, the political balance of the press was fairly evenly divided between the two main political parties, Conservatives and Labour. Individual newspapers were politically partisan, but the *Daily Herald* and the *Daily Mirror* gave the Labour Party a good share of press support. In the early 1970s, newspapers were not, on the whole, extreme in their partisanship. The *Daily Telegraph*, which was a Conservative supporting paper, was not particularly hostile to Labour politicians. The *Daily Mirror*, a Labour supporter, was sympathetic to Heath's Conservative government.

After 1975, commercial and political factors led to much greater partisanship in the press, and by the 1979 election, the majority of newspapers supported the Conservative Party, including the *Sun*, which had previously been the *Daily Herald/Sun*, a staunch supporter of Labour. By the 1992 election, one study showed a bias in the press towards the Conservative Party of about 43 percentage points, as against a gap of 8 per cent between the voters.[2] The importance of political bias in the press needs to be looked at in the context of the British electoral system. The 'first past the post' system means that a party can win a massive parliamentary majority on a very small percentage win over their opponents. Small swings in support can have major consequences for election results. As the *Sun* itself said after the 1992 election: IT'S THE SUN WOT WON IT!

However, the position changed in 1997 when New Labour won a landslide victory. Newspaper support for political parties had changed. Did this influence the outcome of the election? In 1997, New Labour was supported by the *Guardian*, the *Independent*, the *Financial Times*, the *Daily Mirror*, the *Sun* and the *Daily Star*. The Conservatives were supported by the *Daily Telegraph*, the *Daily Express*, and the *Daily Mail*. *The Times* was relatively neutral. A survey carried out after polling day showed a correlation between voting behaviour and newspaper readership, though the extent to which voters were influenced by the stance taken by newspapers is not clear.

In the 2001 election, New Labour again gained more newspaper support than the Conservatives. In a low turnout, they won with a large majority.

The problem of bias in the press is not a matter of who, or of what system, is supported. The problem is that the bias exists, and the system through which our press operates seems guaranteed to ensure that bias will continue. A mature, healthy democracy needs a system that will allow members of that democracy to decide freely and in an informed manner by what system they want to live. If people are not given the information, it is difficult for them to exercise their choices appropriately.

In the meantime, it is important that readers of newspapers become critical readers, who are aware of, and can identify, gaps and swings in the information they are given. This book is designed to help that process.

Notes

1   The classification is taken from Tunstall 1996.
2   ibid. pp. 240–241.

Headlines

WHAT IS A HEADLINE?

The headline is a unique type of text. It has a range of functions that specifically dictate its shape, content and structure, and it operates within a range of restrictions that limit the freedom of the writer. For example, the space that the headline will occupy is almost always dictated by the layout of the page, and the size of the typeface will similarly be restricted. The headline will rarely, if ever, be written by the reporter who wrote the news story. It should, in theory, encapsulate the story in a minimum number of words, attract the reader to the story and, if it appears on the front page, attract the reader to the paper.

This mix of functions immediately presents a problem: headlines can often, in their attempt to attract a reader to a story, be ambiguous or confusing. This unit looks at the function of headlines, and the linguistic and graphological devices that headline writers use to create headlines that are effective.

WHAT ARE HEADLINES FOR?

Newspapers are ephemeral texts, that is, they are intended only for the day they are delivering the news. They cater for a wide range of readers with a wide range of needs. Some people may read the paper thoroughly, taking in every aspect; others, probably the majority, skip certain sections and read others in more detail. Some may read only one section. And, of course, each reader may change his/her mode of reading depending on the demands of the day. The headline has the capacity to encapsulate a story, and the headlines in a particular edition give the reader the overall picture of the current news (headline content), its relative importance (visual impact and position in the paper), its classification (which section of the paper it's in – sports, finance, overseas news, etc.). In theory, then, the reader can skim the headlines and have an outline of the news of the day, and some idea of its relative impact and importance. The question is, to what extent do headlines actually work in this way?

Activity

Here is a selection of headlines from a range of newspapers from 30 September 2001. They are in random order, and not classified according to newspaper.

◎ Can you tell, from the headline, what the story is about?
◎ If you were an editor, which of these stories would you put on the front page of your paper?
◎ Which would be your lead (most important) story?

Compare your answers with someone else's. How much agreement is there?

Text: Headlines

1	NO HIDING PLACE FOR TERRORISTS
2	BILL TAKES HIS GIRL TO OXFORD
3	FIRE FIGHT
4	BUS STOP DAD KILLED AS HE SAVES HIS LAD
3	PUPIL SUES SCHOOL AFTER FAILING LATIN
4	POSH TURNS UP AS SUITABLE CELEBRITY
7	INTO THE WAR ZONE
8	HOPES RISE FOR OUR REPORTER CAPTURED BY TALIBAN
9	I'LL KNOCK IT ALL ON THE ED, MAMA

Commentary

These headlines come from six national newspapers. Stories 1, 3 and 7 relate to the terrorist attack on the USA that took place on 11 September 2001. All the newspapers devoted a large amount of space to aspects of this story which was a lead story in four, and a front page story in five.

Story 4 appears in only two papers as an important inside story in one and a news short in another.

Story 5 appears in four papers, as a small inside story in two, and an important inside story in two.

Story 8 appeared in all the papers, and as a lead story in one.

Stories 2, 6 and 9 have headlines that are difficult to understand without the accompanying article. Story 2 refers to Chelsea Clinton's arrival at Oxford accompanied by her father, and appeared in all the papers, and as a front page story in one. Story 6 refers to Victoria Beckham (Posh Spice) attending a fashion show and appeared as an important inside story in one paper. Story 9 refers to the filming by Prince Edward's TV company 'Ardent' of his nephew, Prince William and the subsequent row. This story appeared as an important inside story in all the papers.

A quick look across the headlines like this makes it clear that headlines are of limited use in giving a clear overview on the news of the day, or the relative importance of the items.

Did you, as an individual, agree with the importance given to the main stories, and was there agreement within the group? If there were disagreements, what did they revolve around?

THE LANGUAGE OF HEADLINES

This section looks at the language and structure of headlines.

Rapping, slamming, probing and blasting: the vocabulary of the headline writer

Over time, headline writers have developed a vocabulary that fulfils the requirements of the headline, using words that are short, attention getting and effective. Many of the words that are 'typical' of the headline are probably rarely found outside this particular text type. A few may move from the headline into a wider field.

Activity

Try to find one word to replace the words and phrases in the following list, that would be appropriate to use in a headline.

To reprimand or tell off; to follow someone or to be pursued by someone or something; someone who is claiming state benefits; a person who has behaved dishonourably; excellent or first class; to defeat soundly; to investigate; political corruption; to increase rapidly; to decrease rapidly; an informer or to inform; people with left-wing political beliefs; to criticize strongly; to make a strong commitment or promise.

Commentary

Words you may have used include rap, dog, scrounger, rat, crack (or ace), thrash, probe, sleaze, spiral or soar, slump, grass, lefties or reds, slam or blast, vow.

Are all newspapers likely to use these words in their headlines? The examples below suggest that the majority are widely used, but that scrounger, rat, lefties and reds are more likely to be found in tabloid newspapers rather than broadsheet publications.

PUTTING WORDS IN: WHAT THE HEADLINE WRITER INCLUDES

The majority of the headline words looked at in the previous section are not chosen just as devices to use space economically. They also have the effect of being attention getting. The headline writer has a range of linguistic devices available to create headlines that will attract the reader's interest.

Activity

In each of the following groups of headlines, certain words and phrases have been highlighted. Can you suggest why these particular words have been used? What effect is created?

Group 1

1 **AISLE** NOT MARRY YOU
2 UP BEFORE THE **BEAK** – PECKISH SWAN GIVES MICHAEL BARRYMORE A NASTY NIP
3 LABOUR **BANKS** ON CELEBRITY SUPPORT
4 **TITANIC** KATE GOES ON DIET

Group 2

1 **BRULEE MADLY DEEPLY**
2 **SUPER CALLY GO BALLISTIC CELTIC ARE ATROCIOUS**
3 **EAGLE IS LANDED**
4 JOIN THE KEW FOR **THE BLOOM WITH A PHEW**

Group 3

1 **STUPID SOPHIE** GAGGED BY THE PALACE
2 **HIT AND MYTH**
3 EDWARD FACES A **ROASTING AT ROYAL** MEETING
4 **TONY'S PHONEY**-WAR CABINET

Group 4

1 'COVER-UP' **OUTCRY** OVER FOOT-AND-MOUTH **PROBE**
2 THE STREETS OF **CARNAGE**
3 GENIUS REV **BUTCHERED** AT CHURCH
4 DYING SUE'S CANCER **RAP**

Commentary

Headline writers use a range of language devices to make their headlines memorable and striking. These groups each give examples of some of these devices in action.

Word and meaning: Group 1

All the headlines in group 1 play on the potential for ambiguity that can exist in the relationship between word and meaning. For example, the word *aisle* is a **homophone** (i.e. is identical in sound) of the phrase *I'll*.

Headline 3, a story about the funding of the Labour party contains an ambiguous use of the word *bank*. The word is a **polyseme** (i.e. has several closely related meanings). It can be a noun meaning an establishment where money is deposited – but it can also be a verb meaning to depend on – the factual meaning required by the story. A serious social issue is therefore headlined by a linguistic joke. Headline 2 makes use of the fact that the word *beak* is a **homonym** (i.e. it has more than one meaning, and these meanings are not obviously related). It can mean the jaws of a bird, but it is also a slang term for magistrate or judge. Michael Barrymore has been attacked by a swan, but he is also facing a criminal investigation. Headline 4 makes use of metaphorical associations. *Titanic* means 'of enormous size', but it also refers to the film of that name, in which actress Kate Winslett starred. Winslett had recently been in the news because she had gained weight.

Intertextuality: Group 2

Any culture will have a range of familiar phrases and sayings, and in the case of our particular culture, many of these come from popular songs, films, book titles, etc. Headline writers often make reference to these, as in the examples in group 2. For example, Headline 1 refers to a well-known film, *Truly, Madly, Deeply*. Headline 2 makes a reference to a nonsense word that was coined for the children's film, *Mary Poppins*, supercalifraga-listicexpialidocious. Headline 3 make reference to the title of a well-known novel: Jack Higgins' *The Eagle has Landed*.

Phonology: Group 3

Though headlines are written to be read, not spoken, a very common way of making headlines memorable is to use the reader's awareness of sound. Headlines 1 and 3 use alliteration on /s/ and /r/, and headline 2 uses the phonological similarity between **myth** and **miss** to make reference to the phrase hit and miss. Headline 4 uses the rhyme of 'Tony' and 'Phoney' to create a memorable headline and perhaps to make political comment.

Loaded words: Group 4

In order to make headlines attract the attention of the reader, headline writers may select words that carry particularly strong connotations, that is, carry an emotional loading beyond their literal meaning. A good example in the data is the word **butchered** in headline 2. This word has the dictionary meaning of *to slaughter and cut up an animal*. When it is applied to a human being, it carries both the meaning of extreme and cruel violence, and also implies that the killer must have seen the victim as having the same status as an animal.

TAKING WORDS OUT: WHAT THE HEADLINE WRITER OMITS

Activity

Look at the following headlines, and rewrite them in clear standard English, by adding any missing words. Try not to make any other changes.

PARAS FLY TO BATTLE ZONE
LAGS BLOCK CUSHY JOB FOR ARCHER
CRASH CAUSED BY FAULTY BRAKES
HIGH SCORE SAVES BOOKIES PACKET
JUVENILE COURT TO TRY SHOOTING DEFENDANTS

What classes of words are headline writers likely to omit, and why?

Commentary

The words you might have added to the headlines include *the, a, are, were, is* and often titles such as *Mr., Sir, Lord*, etc. The headline writer needs to include the factual detail of the story in a way that will attract the reader's attention. Given that space is limited, lexical words (words that have meaning, such as nouns, main verbs, adjectives, adverbs) are far more useful to the writer than grammatical words (words that signal grammatical relationships, such as determiners – *the, a, this, that*, etc., auxiliary verbs *be, have, do*). But this can occasionally lead to ambiguity, as many lexical words depend on grammatical words to establish which word class they are. This can lead to headlines such as:

1   BRITISH LEFT WAFFLES ON FALKLAND ISLANDS
2   LUNG CANCER IN WOMEN MUSHROOMS
3   RED TAPE HOLDS UP NEW BRIDGE
4   POLICE BEGIN CAMPAIGN TO RUN DOWN JAYWALKERS
5   KIDS MAKE NUTRITIOUS SNACKS
6   PROSTITUTES APPEAL TO POPE
7   SQUAD HELPS DOG BITE VICTIM

19

The reader is left floundering as the meaning is almost irretrievably ambiguous until the accompanying article is read. The first two headlines are difficult to interpret because the word class of 'left' and 'mushrooms' isn't clear, and the context leads the reader towards the wrong choice. The reader is likely to make the obvious interpretation of 'British left' as **Subject** and **Verb** in a sentence. However, it is intended as a noun phrase. The word 'mushroom' is most frequently used as a noun. This expectation leads the reader to see 'women mushrooms' as a noun phrase. In this case, 'mushrooms' is being used as a verb, giving the structure:

S	V
Lung cancer in women	mushrooms

In headlines 3 and 4, the ambiguity is caused by the different possible meanings of the phrases 'hold up' and 'run down'. Something similar is happening in headline 6. It is not possible to tell whether the verb used is the phrasal verb 'appeal to' or the single verb 'appeal'.

In headline 5, the ambiguity occurs because of the different, but closely linked meanings of 'make'.

In headline 7, it is impossible to tell if 'dog bite victim' is a noun phrase. In the headline, it looks more like a noun followed by a verb and direct object.

SHAKING IT ALL ABOUT: HOW THE HEADLINE WRITER REORGANISES LANGUAGE

In order to produce punchy, economical texts, the headline writer also plays about with the standard order of words and phrases.

Activity

Look at the following headlines. Try to rewrite the highlighted sections in clear standard English.

1   EASTER AT RISK IN **SIX-TERM SHAKE-UP** FOR THE SCHOOL YEAR
2   **TEST TUBE BABY PIONEER** ACCUSED OF MISCONDUCT
3   **DRUGLINK FEAR** AS DEAD PAIR NAMED
4   FAN BANNED OVER **TERROR TAUNT CLAIM**
5   **'BANDIT' CAR CHASE POLICE INSTRUCTOR** FINED £750 AFTER DEATH OF NURSE

Nouns form patterns with other words to form noun phrases. A noun phrase will always contain a noun. The shortest possible noun phrase consists of a single noun, e.g. *cars*, *people*. The main noun in a noun phrase is called the **headword**. Noun phrases can also contain determiners – *the*, *a*, *these*, etc., producing a two-word noun phrase: *these cars*, *the people*, *a pensioner*. More information can be included in the noun phrase by adding a **modifier** between the determiner and the noun: *these fast cars*, *the important people*, *an angry pensioner*. Noun phrases can have more than one modifier, *these fast sports cars*, *the important political people*, *the angry Yorkshire pensioners*. Modifiers can add various kinds of information about a noun, including descriptive detail – *blue sky*, *the sweet perfume*, *a misty morning*; number – *the three people*; kind or type – *Yorkshire pensioners*.

Headline writers often put information into the modifier slot in the noun phrase, to produce a form of shorthand that is a very distinctive feature of newspaper style. For example, the story covered by headline 5 is about a police driving instructor involved in a fatal car crash when he was chasing another car as part of a training exercise. This fairly complex piece of information is encapsulated in a long noun phrase. The phrase **police instructor** gives information about the person responsible for the accident. The phrase **car chase**, used to modify police instructor, gives the event, and the word **bandit**, graphologically marked with inverted commas to indicate that this was not a real police chase, gives the context in which the event took place.

Many words have the capacity to **class-shift**, that is, to operate as more than one word class. For example, **chase** can be either a noun or a verb, **a chase** or **to chase**. By using chase as a noun in headline 5, the writer manages to include the action – chase – without having to include it as a verb. Some headlines omit the verb completely by implying the action within the noun phrase. The capacity the noun phrase has for modification makes this particular structure a very flexible one, and therefore extremely useful to the headline writer.

Activity

Here are three news stories, outlined briefly in standard English. Turn each one into a single noun phrase that would make an appropriate headline, and label modifiers and the headword for each noun phrase. The first one has been done as an example.

◎   A Labrador, Daisy, has had to have emergency veterinary treatment after she ate a daffodil.

◎　　A man who killed two pensioners when he attempted to steal their money has escaped from custody.

◎　　The local police are investigating a teacher's house as they believe she has been running a brothel on the premises.

A possible headline for the first story would be: DAFFY DAISY'S VET-DASH PANIC

mod	*mod*	*headword*
(DAFFY DAISY'S)	VET-DASH	PANIC

Activity

You now have a list of devices that are used by headline writers to create effective headlines.

◎　　Word choice
◎　　Word play
◎　　Intertextuality
◎　　Sound
◎　　Loaded language
◎　　Omission of grammatical words
◎　　Noun phrases
◎　　Class shift

Using one or more of the following texts for the factual details of your story, write three headlines. Try to use each device at least once.

Text 1

> Hey diddle diddle, the cat and the fiddle
> The cow jumped over the moon
> The little dog laughed to see such fun
> And the dish ran away with the spoon

Text 2

Tom-Tom the piper's son
Stole a pig and away did run
The pig was eat
Tom was beat
Tom went roaring down the street

Text 3

There was a young man of high rank
Who went to sea in a tank
They said 'It is sad,
He surely is mad!'
And he proved they were right when he sank.

Text 4

There was a young man from Japan
Whose poetry never would scan
When they asked him why
He said with a sigh,
'It's because I put as many words into the last line as I possibly can.'

Swap your headlines with another group. Can they link your headlines with the correct story?

GRAPHOLOGICAL FEATURES OF HEADLINES

Headlines also have a visual function. The print is larger than the text of the main articles they refer to, but front page headlines, particularly in tabloid newspapers, can by themselves occupy more space than the whole article they refer to.

Headlines work in conjunction with the other visual aspects of the newspaper text, in particular the pictures. A story about a plane crash used the headline AND THEY ALL LIVED. This only carries meaning because it was accompanied by a picture of the crashed plane. The example below (p. 25) operates in a similar way, except that the headline is not completely obscure without the picture – but the picture adds an extra dimension of meaning!

HEADLINES AS INFORMATION

The conflicting roles of the headline – to carry information and to attract the attention of the reader – were discussed briefly above (p. 13). This section looks at the way the headline delivers information, and what, from the point of view of the headline writer, the information actually is in relation to the story.

If a relatively simple definition of information is used, the headline should deliver some detail on what happened, who was involved, where it happened, what the circumstances were. This can be simplified into **what**, **who**, **where**, **how**. Most models of information would include a when and a why element, but as daily newspapers tend to deal with the immediate events, the when can generally be understood. The why tends to be addressed in the article rather than the headline. To what extent, then, do headlines perform this what-where-who-how function?

Activity

The following headlines all appeared on 14 August 1996, and relate to the same story. Take each headline individually and decide

◎ What information does each headline give you?
◎ What are the most important areas of information as far as this headline writer is concerned?

1 LUCKY ESCAPE AS PLANE SKIDS ONTO MOTORWAY
2 AND THEY ALL LIVED
3 ACTRESS LISA'S AMAZING JET CRASH ESCAPE
4 FOUR GOT OUT OF THIS ALIVE
5 CLEESE'S FILM PAL IN PLANE CRASH ESCAPE
6 CLEESE GIRL JET MIRACLE

Diana's fingers do the talking

New beginning: Diana, Princess of Wales leaves an English National Ballet lunch appointment yesterday

Commentary

Analysing headline language from a **what, who, where, how** model (the **wh-model**) presents immediate difficulties, because the headline is not necessarily an independent text, and also the structure of the language may be non-standard. Identifying **who** is not difficult, but **what** can be more of a problem. In most contexts, this would be represented by a verb. Headlines may not contain a verb. The action is frequently nominalised (turned into a noun), which can distance the word or phrase from the actual action. It may be useful here to try to draw from the headlines some factual information and reconstruct the story, which is as follows:

> A plane crashed onto a motorway. Four people were on board. Luckily, no one died.

The information from the headlines above can now be shown like this:

Actors/ participants	Action	Location of action	Other
			circumstances / comment
plane	skids, (escape)	onto motorway	lucky escape
they all	lived		
actress Lisa	(escape), (crash)		amazing jet crash escxape
four	got out	this	alive
Cleese's film			
pal	(escape), (crash)		plane crash escape
Cleese girl			jet miracle

Note: The bracketed words make reference to actions, but are not verbs in the headlines.

How do these headlines work as carriers of information from the wh-model? Headline 1 uses the inanimate 'plane', and allows the reader to make the assumption, to presuppose, that there were passengers and crew aboard.

Headlines 2 and 4 use **deictic reference**, that is reference that depends on the context for its meaning. Deictic language can be defined as language that points, that requires either shared knowledge or an external reference. 'Meet me here at this time tomorrow' only works if addresser and addressee know where 'here' is, and what time 'this time' is.

Similarly, a note on a door saying 'back in 10 minutes' means nothing to the reader unless he or she knows what time it was when the writer left. Reference of this kind is deictic. The examples here, headlines 2 and 4, require a photograph to give meaning to the words **they**, **this**, and **four**.

Headlines 3, 5 and 6 give the reader specific but incomplete or misleading information. 'Lisa', 'Cleese's film pal' and 'Cleese girl' give information about one participant. However, another participant emerges in two of these headlines, actor and writer John Cleese. From an information point of view, this is wasted space, because John Cleese was not involved in any way in this incident. The information that 'Lisa' is an actress could also be seen as secondary to the facts of the event. These headlines direct the reader away from the event and towards the area of media celebrity.

These headlines are, therefore, not very efficient in giving the reader **who** information.

If **what** in the model is considered as the verb element, **what happened**, similar devices are used. Headline 1 uses direct reference to action: skids. In all the other headlines, the reference is indirect. It will be useful here to look at the structure of the phrases used to represent the action in headlines 3, 5 and 6.

In each case, the event of the crash is nominalised, that is, turned into a noun. Instead of using a structure such as PLANE CRASHES, these headline writers have chosen to use noun phrases: 'amazing jet crash escape', 'plane crash escape', 'jet miracle'. Headline 6 removes the idea of a crash altogether, and in headlines 3 and 5, the headword, the main focus of the noun phrase, is the word 'escape'. The word 'crash' is used in a position of less focus, as a modifier in the noun phrase.

In headlines 2 and 4, the reference to the crash is deictic, that is, dependent on the context. The action relates to the event of survival: 'lived' and 'got out'.

The **what** element is, therefore, focused very much on the fact that people survived this particular accident, rather than on the fact that the accident itself happened.

If **how** is taken to cover circumstance, then the headlines also deal with this. It is unusual for there to be any survivors of a plane crash, and this is the circumstance that the headline writers focus on, directly in the case of headlines 1, 3 and 6 that use the words 'lucky', 'amazing' and 'miracle'; and by linking with the graphology in headlines 2 and 4. Headline 5 confines itself to the use of the word 'escape', which, combined with 'jet crash', implies a lucky escape.

The where and when elements are largely ignored. Headline 1 gives the information that the plane crashed onto a motorway, the other headlines ignore this.

There is, therefore, very little consensus about the 'facts' surrounding this news story. All the papers agree on the importance of the 'luck' element, but only three of them inform the reader of the fact that no one was killed. The other three only give this information about one passenger. Headline 1 gives 'luck' information, the fact that the plane skidded, and the information about the motorway. Headlines 2 and 4 concentrate on the luck element alone. Headline 3 focuses on one passenger, an actress, and headlines 5 and 6 concentrate on actor and writer John Cleese, who was not actually involved in the event.

HEADLINES AS OPINION MANIPULATORS

Headlines have a persuasive function when they are designed to attract the attention of the reader and interest him/her in reading the story (or in the case of front page headlines, in buying the newspaper), but they can also be written to influence the opinion of the reader. After the death of the Princess of Wales, newspapers became a lot more cautious about intruding into the privacy of the royal family, particularly that of Prince William and Prince Harry. When Prince William started university, the newspapers were given a photo-opportunity, and then agreed to leave the prince alone. However, Ardent Films, the company owned by Prince Edward, Prince William's uncle, continued to film around the university, and allegedly interviewed students about Prince William. The newspapers, the tabloids in particular, fell on this story with glee.

This is an interesting story from a newspaper point of view, not just for its royal content which always excites the tabloids, but because it allowed the papers to comment obliquely on Prince William as a student, and also to occupy the moral high ground from which they had been excluded for some time. The story also gave the papers the chance to rehash the 'royal soap'. Effectively, newspaper readers were asked to take sides between Prince Edward and Prince Charles. However, there were more important issues raised by this story. Some members of the royal family had been criticised for apparently using their connections as a business advantage. Prince Edward's wife, the Countess of Wessex had recently been involved in a scandal around this issue, and some commentators felt that the problem had been brushed under the carpet. This story revived the issue which had previously been a matter of some division between the Prince of Wales and Prince Edward.

Newspaper		Headline
Sun	1	STUPID SOPHIE GAGGED BY THE PALACE
	2	EDWARD GOES SHOOTING AS THE WORLD MOURNS
	3	HE'S A LAW UNTO HIMSELF
Daily Mail/Mail on Sunday	4	I GOT IT WRONG OVER WILLS, SAYS EDWARD
Daily Mirror/Sunday Mirror	5	NOT SO FAST MS BOND
	6	DAFT UNCLE ED STRIKES AGAIN
	7	SAY SORRY . . . NOW
	8	YOU F***ING IDIOT
	9	CAN IT, EDWARD
	10	QUEEN SAYS: NO MORE ROYAL SHOWS
	11	I'LL KNOCK IT ALL ON THE ED, MAMA
Independent on Sunday	12	'DIM' EDWARD GIVES TABLOIDS THE LAST LAUGH
News of the World	13	ANGRY EDWARD HAS US NICKED
	14	£50 A HEAD TO LIE ABOUT WILLS
	15	10 WAYS THEY CAN SAVE THEIR MONEY
Observer	16	EDWARD TO TELL QUEEN: NO MORE ROYAL FILMS

How do these headlines represent the protagonists in this story, and to what extent are the constitutional implications of this story addressed?

Activity

For each of the newspapers quoted, list the names or pronouns used to refer to:

> Prince William
> Prince Edward
> The Countess of Wessex
> The Prince of Wales
> The Queen
> Other

What attitudes does the naming suggest to each of the protagonists involved?

29

Commentary

Prince Edward appears in several of the headlines as 'Edward', 'Uncle Ed', 'I', 'he', 'himself', 'you'. The Countess of Wessex, his wife, appears as 'Sophie', and the couple appear as 'they'. The Queen is named as 'Queen', 'mama'. Prince William is 'Wills'. Prince Charles is not named. Other direct protagonists are palace officials: 'the palace'. However, other protagonists appear in these stories. There is reference to 'the world' in recognition of the recent terror strikes in the USA, to the BBC's royal correspondent, Jenni Bond: 'Ms Bond'. The News of the World involves itself in the story: 'us', and the *Independent* refers to newspaper involvement, though apparently excluding itself from the group: 'tabloids'

The focus of the story is, therefore, Prince Edward. Though the naming strategies adopted may appear friendly – first name, nickname – they are in fact hostile. The name is modified by adjectives such as 'stupid', 'daft' and 'dim'. The short form 'Ed' is not one used by the prince or his family, it is imposed informality by the newspapers and denotes a lack of respect. Prince William, on the other hand, is named by his family nickname, 'Wills', indicating a friendly or sympathetic response.

Activity

The naming devices used in the headlines suggest that the papers are unsympathetic towards Prince Edward. Can you identify other language devices that have this effect? Does the headline represent the spoken voice? Who is 'speaking'? Who is addressed by the headline? How are the protagonists described or represented?

Commentary

In the *Sun* and the *Mirror*, the 'voice' of the royal entourage is apparently heard: 'He's a law unto himself', 'Not so fast Ms Bond'. The first comment is critical and relates to the prince's apparent ignoring of the recent tragedy. The second shows him as overbearing when his 'minder' removes a BBC reporter from a royal visit. The 'voices' of Prince Edward and Prince Charles are also heard. Prince Edward, who is portrayed as acting arrogantly and defiantly in headlines that use third person reference, is shown as humbled when his 'voice' is given. 'I got it wrong over Wills,' 'No more royal films,' or is portrayed as a figure of fun: 'I'll knock it all on the ed.' Prince Charles' voice is angry and authoritative: 'Say sorry . . . now,'. The attribution of an expletive: 'You f***ing idiot' gives the impression of appropriate anger, and presents Prince Charles as being forthright and plain spoken, in contrast to his evasive brother. The Queen's 'voice' is also heard: 'Can it, Edward', 'No more royal shows.'

The headlines give the story from a range of apparently different perspectives. There is the 'voice' of Prince Edward, the 'voice' of the Prince of Wales, the 'voice' of the Queen, the 'voice' of palace officials and minders. It is easy for the reader to forget, or to fail to recognise, that the actual perspective is that of the newspaper. Similarly, the person or people addressed are assumed to share the perspective that the paper offers. The reader may or may not, in fact, share this perspective. The paper therefore creates another participant in the story – an '**implied reader**' to whom the text is addressed.

	Actual voice	Implied voice	Actual recipient	Implied recipient
(1, 2, 6, 12, 13, 14, 15)	paper	paper	reader	Implied reader
(3, 5)	paper	officials	reader	Implied reader/ Jennie Bond
(4, 11, 16)	paper	Prince Edward	reader	Palace/queen
(7, 8)	paper	Prince Charles	reader	Prince Edward
(9, 10)	paper	Queen	reader	Prince Edward

The headlines also exclude, or reduce the importance of other perspectives, by the way the headlines are structured. Though several protagonists are included in the headlines, Prince Edward is more frequently placed in the subject position, often as the **theme** of the clause sentence. (For a discussion of theme, see p. 85 below).

Subject	Verb	Complement	Direct object	Adverbial	Indirect object
Edward	goes shooting			as the world mourns	
He	's	a law unto himself			
Edward	says		I got it wrong Over Wills		
Daft Uncle Ed	strikes			again	
'Dim' Edward	gives		the last laugh		tabloids

The overall effect is to present the reader with one point of view to the exclusion of any other. The headlines present Edward as arrogant, aloof and unintelligent, a suitable target for derision and ridicule. His brother, by contrast, is straightforward and strong. It is interesting to contrast the papers' attitude – particularly the tabloids' attitude – to Prince Charles in comparison to the hostility shown towards him at the time of his divorce.

Summary

Headlines are important in their own right. They are the first text that a newspaper reader sees when buying and reading the paper. They employ a range of creative language devices to produce short, attention-getting, highly memorable texts, and have the capacity to encapsulate an entire story in a few words.

This Unit has looked at some of the devices the headline writer uses to create effective headlines – sound via alliteration, homophones and rhyme; word and meaning via naming, loaded language, ambiguity and word play; syntax via the use of structures designed to focus on specific aspects of the text; non-standard structures, omission of words to create a telegraphic style. Headline writers also use selection of information; and direct and indirect address to readers or other participants in the story.

Lastly, but as importantly, headlines use graphology, the visual aspect of text, to draw the reader's eye. If you, as the reader are visually attracted to a text, and then enticed by an ambiguous or startling text, the newspaper has

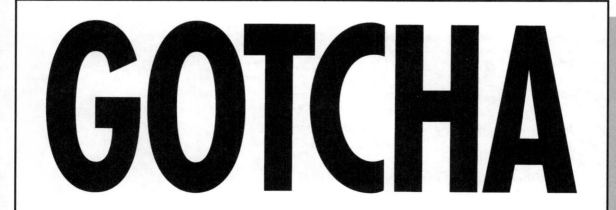

1   Look up newspaper headlines on the internet. Try some of the addresses on pp 111–113 below. Do they follow the patterns identified in this unit?

2   Collect and analyse the front page headlines of several newspapers: broadsheet, tabloid and local. Are there any differences between individual newspapers or between types of newspaper?

3   Collect examples of headlines from newspapers of 30 years ago. (Your local library should have back copies of *The Times* on micro-film.) Have headlines changed in the last 30 years? Look at earlier newspapers as well.

4   These headlines appeared in the American newspaper (*Chicago Tribune*, *The New York Times*, *International Herald Tribune*). Do these headlines use similar devices to those found in the British press?

ANTI-AIRCRAFT GUNS OPEN UP AROUND AFGHANISTAN
    CAPITAL AS HIGH FLYING PLANES PASS OVERHEAD?
GIRL SCOUTS TAKE ON THE HUNTERS NEXT DOOR
RAISING MUNICH, SHARON REVEALS ISRAELI QUALMS
U.S. AND BRITAIN MAKE LATE PUSH TO FORGE COALITION
    FOR COMBAT
FOR WASHINGTON, A MODERN PEARL HARBOR
WORLD AIR TRAFFIC TURNS CHAOTIC

Audience

The audience for a newspaper is its reader. This may seem to be too obvious to state, but it raises some important points about the way papers relate to their audience, and the difference between the 'real' audience, the readership, and the audience the paper appears to be writing for – the 'implied' audience. This unit looks at the way newspapers assume the existence of groups that may not actually exist as groups within society and, by addressing themselves to these groups, create a shared ideology that can frequently work to obscure issues rather than clarify them.

WHO READS THE PAPERS?

Newspaper groups do market research and are well aware of the profile of their readership. There are certain assumptions that people tend to make about newspaper readerships: *Sun* readers are supposed to be Tory supporters, and working-class; *Guardian* readers are expected to be left-wing, middle-class, Labour supporters; *Sun* readers are supposed to be younger, *Telegraph* readers older, but these labels are not really very useful or even very accurate.

Surveys done in 1995 show that the *Daily Telegraph* and the *Daily Express* had fewer younger readers (aged 15–44 years) than the *Guardian* and the *Daily Star*. The *Daily Telegraph*, *The Times*, the *Independent* and the

Guardian had a high percentage (over 70 per cent) of middle class – ABC1 readers, the *Daily Express* and the *Daily Mail* had over 60 per cent ABC1 readers, and the *Daily Mirror*, the *Sun* and the *Daily Star* had over 20 per cent ABC1 readers. At this time, 65 per cent of the readers of both the *Guardian* and the *Daily Star* were aged between 15 and 44 years (Tunstall, 1996, p. 93).

In 1995, a survey showed that 61 per cent of the readership of the *Sun* expressed a preference for Labour (ibid, p. 242).

Activity

Do a quick survey around (1) your group, and (2) your college. Find out who reads what paper, and see if you can identify patterns of readership for particular papers according to age, gender, political sympathies, social class, age.

Commentary

It is unlikely that you are able to profile, from such a survey, a 'typical' *Sun* reader, or a 'typical' *Times* reader. Newspaper readerships tend to be diverse, and you would need to look at large numbers to find any very significant patterns.

HOW NEWSPAPERS IDENTIFY THEIR AUDIENCE

There may be no clear profile of a '*Sun* reader' or a '*Guardian* reader', but the papers themselves often write as though such a person exists and that there is, in fact, a homogeneous group of people with shared beliefs and values whose defining feature is the newspaper that they read.

In the article 'Hula Meanie', '*Sun* readers' are explicitly identified as a group. The article reports that they voted 5–1 in favour of a particular outcome (who is entitled to a prize). The person against whom the '*Sun* readers' voted is a 'meanie', and 'defiant'. Under his photograph he is quoted as saying 'it's not fair'. He 'spurns' and 'snubbed' *Sun* readers.

There are several contexts here. The language of a child's experience is used – 'meanie', 'It's not fair'. These terms are applied to the 'opponent' of the readers. The implication is that his behaviour is childish, and therefore possibly unreasonable. The use of the terms 'spurn' and 'snubbed' imply disdain, contempt and rebuff. The prize money is described as 'loot' – with the implication of ill-gotten gains.

HULA MEANIE SPURNS SUN READERS ON LOOT

DEFIANT Steve Maxwell last night snubbed Sun readers by refusing to give a £10,000 Hula Hoops prize to the boy who found it.

Meanie Steve claimed: "I'm being made to look the bad guy and it's just not fair." He has offered £1,800 to 11-year-old Christopher Wright.

But in a weekend You the Jury poll Sun readers voted 5–1 that Christopher and his family should get all the loot.

Christopher found the winning "Twister" Hula Hoop in a 24p packet Steve's wife Jackie gave him. He said Jackie promised him £5,000.

Now parents Gordon and Bernadette are taking legal action.

But Steve, 37, of Wyken, West Midlands,

Steve . . . "it's not fair"

EXCLUSIVE by ANDREW PARKER

said: "It will take a court to make me hand over £5,000.

"Jackie bought the Hula Hoops and they were her property."

And mum-of-four Jackie added: "Bernadette was a friend of mine but not anymore."

The person who opposes the '*Sun* readers' is, therefore, by implication, childish, unreasonable, ill-mannered and dishonest. *Sun* readers are, also by implication, against these qualities, and for maturity, fair play, courtesy and honesty.

The '*Sun* readers', however, are not clearly defined. Who exactly voted 5–1 for a particular outcome? Six people? Six hundred people? Six thousand people? This information is not given.

Activity

Look at the extract from the *Daily Mirror*, and answer the questions that follow.

- ◎ How does the article identify its audience?
- ◎ What qualities does this audience have?
- ◎ What qualities do the people who 'oppose' the audience have?
- ◎ What actions does each group perform?
- ◎ What role does the newspaper itself play?

37

Text: Queen

QUEEN SNUBS 102,625

DAILY Mirror READERS

THE Queen has delivered an amazing snub to the Daily Mirror's loyal army of readers.

By LUCY TURNER

Buckingham Palace officials refused to accept our massive petition to win back Princess Diana's HRH status.

An astonishing 102,625 readers have now signed up to our campaign urging the Queen to restore the title.

But when we tried to hand over the letters at the palace gates, we were turned away.

The Mirror arrived in style in a horse-drawn carriage, complete with coachman and footman in full regalia.

Arrest

Inside were three bulging sackfuls of letters.

When we drew up, we were threatened with arrest. Then a stony-faced police officer at the gates told us: "Sorry, we were expecting you a couple of days ago with this and I have been told not to take anything from you."

He even refused to accept a personal letter to the Queen urging her to reconsider her decision to strip the princess of her royal title.

"You will have to post it," the officer said.

"We cannot accept it unless it is by courier or by post."

The Mirror made its first-class delivery after an earlier snub from the palace. Last week we handed in about 200 letters summing up the many thousands we have received. But they were rudely returned in a scruffy brown envelope with no covering letter.

Diana lost her HRH status in her recent divorce settlement with Prince Charles.

The audience is identified in relation to the newspaper read: '*Mirror* readers'. They are identified as 'the *Daily Mirror*'s loyal army of readers'. The metaphoric reference to the readers as an army adds emphasis to the quality of loyalty, but the image is confusing. Are they the Queen's loyal army – in which case her 'snub' becomes particularly bad – or are they the newspaper's loyal army – in which case they are fighting for justice for the Princess of Wales. The role and identity of the readers becomes more confused as it is engulfed in the identity of the newspaper itself. First there is reference to '*our* massive petition', and '*our* campaign', which moves to '*we* tried to hand over the letters'. At this point it is not entirely clear whether 'our' and 'we' represents the editorial stance of the paper alone, or the paper and its readership. Finally, the paper is personified as 'The Mirror arrived in style'. At this point, the paper itself has become a protagonist in the event, rather than a mechanism for reporting it.

The Queen is the opponent in the *Mirror* story. She 'snubs' the readers, and 'delivers an amazing snub'.

The audience for this article is apparently a group who have signed a petition to the Queen and who feel strongly that Princess Diana should retain the title HRH (Her Royal Highness). This group has made an appeal that has been abruptly and rudely rejected. By identifying this audience as '*Mirror* readers', the paper has included all the readers of that article within the group – though many of them may not share the view about the Princess of Wales, and the majority will probably not have signed the petition.

An interesting aspect of this kind of reporting is that a conflict is established between groups and individuals who have never met, or encountered each other in any way. The 'opponents' of the readers have their actions described in ways that imply their hostility towards these non-existent groups. The descriptions of these opponents are generally negative, either through direct description, or through the words used for their actions.

These stories may not relate to fundamentally important issues – particularly the story about the prize money, which amounts to manufactured news. The *Sun* created a poll, and then reported the results. The *Daily Mirror* too has manufactured a story. The news item is clearly one of legitimate national interest – the future status of the Princess of Wales – but this particular item is, again, a paper placing itself within a story where from a news point of view it really has no role.

This kind of audience creation is overt. The paper identifies the group, names it and champions its cause. The reader of the paper, particularly if he/she is a regular reader, becomes part of that group, and may feel that he/she has been 'snubbed' or in some way insulted or ignored. This can help to promote a sense of group homogeneity that does not, in fact, exist.

THE IDENTITY OF THE READER

It is important to distinguish between the reader as an individual who may or may not read that particular newspaper regularly, and the 'created' reader who is being identified in the text. For the purposes of analysis, the reader as individual will be referred to as **the reader**, the created reader will be referred to as **the implied reader**.

Creating a system of shared values

In the examples discussed in the previous section, the appeal to the implied readership is overt. The group is actually named in the story. A more common way in which papers may identify and address their implied readership is by reporting stories in a way that is designed to evoke one particular response, thus establishing a set of shared values, usually in opposition to another group who do not share, or who attack these values.

One obvious area in which newspapers tend to polarise, and thus try to create different sets of shared values, is in the area of party politics (see the discussion of the role of newspapers in the 1992 election in the introduction p. 10) but it is often more revealing to look at attitudes expressed towards other aspects of our culture – for example gender, ethnicity, family, sexual orientation. It has already been suggested in the previous section that newspaper readers as a group do not exist and do not have the uniformity of views on any given range of topics that some news reporting may suggest. How, then, do newspapers create their implied readership and appeal to this sense of shared values that the implied readership is supposed to have? The next section will address this issue.

THE ROLE OF THE AUDIENCE

If there is no such individual as the '*Sun* reader' or the '*Guardian* reader', why is audience an important concept when the language of newspapers is under consideration?

Language always occurs within a context, and as social users of language individuals know how to respond to linguistic triggers relating to the context of the language situation, the intended message, the feedback and input from others. It could be argued that language is the key factor in the establishment and maintenance of social groups, of society as an entity. Language allows individuals to communicate, to interpret the world and themselves, to express logic, causes and outcomes, to establish relationships within the group. Recent studies into the development of language within the individual suggest that the development of the social skills of language is as crucial as the development of the structural aspects of language. Disorders that affect the development of what are referred to as **pragmatic** skills (as found, for example, in many autistic people) are as disabling as disorders that affect the development at a structural level.

Activity

Look at the following transcripts of language that took place in a variety of contexts. At first glance, these utterances look strange – responses seem irrelevant, statements over-obvious, but all of these exchanges worked, in that all participants understood the intended meaning of the utterance. Can you account for this?

(*Two students*)
A: Are you going to Davo's tonight?
B.   It's Thursday.

(*Group of students in a joke-telling session*)
A: How many surrealists does it take to paint a house?
B: Fish.

(*Lecturer and student*)
L: There's a problem with this video.
S: It works better if you plug it in.

(*Student to student*)
A: Where's the pen?
B.   Where's your glasses?

Commentary

As individuals and as members of groups, we assume that language contains meaning, and we conduct exchanges with that assumption as an important factor. We tend to look for meaning where it may initially appear to be missing. One possible reason why proof-reading a piece of written text is so difficult is that the reader tends to see what he/she expects to be there rather than what is.

Each of these exchanges appears initially to break the rules of meaning. In the first two exchanges, the response seems to be irrelevant. The third one seems to be a classic case of stating the obvious and the fourth one again seems irrelevant because instead of answering the question the second participant responds with another question. However, most people have no problems in sorting these exchanges out.

In the first exchange, it is clear that both parties are aware of some event that happens on Thursdays (or on that particular Thursday) that makes the proposed visit impossible. As they are both aware of this, there is no need to clarify the situation beyond the reminder that is issued – it's Thursday. Any further information would be irrelevant. The second exchange is a joke that plays on the fact that we expect meaning in language. Surrealists by definition operate beyond the expected parameters of meaning, so a totally irrelevant answer completes the joke, which is one of a series of jokes that operates to the same question/answer structure. The third exchange apparently offers unnecessary information, but is, in fact, carrying an implication. The information offered is that a particular piece of equipment isn't plugged in, but a further comment is contained in the way the remark is phrased – the addressee has made a foolish mistake. The fourth exchange operates in a similar way. The reply, apparently irrelevant, carries the information that the addresser hasn't looked closely enough.

There are a whole range of contextual triggers that allow a range of messages to be carried in discourse. These messages, as noted above, help to maintain social role and cohesion. Newspapers function within a social context, and operate, of necessity, within the language framework. By using the social aspects of language, newspapers begin to establish a group identity within the readership.

Activity

Text: Poem fury is part of an article that appeared in the *Daily Mail*, and refers to a planned broadcast of Tony Harrison's poem, 'V'. How does this text place an implied reader within a context that suggests a system of shared values?

◎ What emotional context are the writers trying to establish? What emotion do they require of their readers? How does the text achieve this?

◎ Who is opposing the broadcast, and how does the text indicate this?

◎ What, do you assume, is the subject matter of the poem? What leads you to this assumption?

FOUR-LETTER TV POEM FURY

By JOHN DEANS and GARRY JENKINS

BROADCASTERS are lining up for a head-on clash with the political establishment over a planned Channel 4 programme featuring a
5 **torrent of fourletter filth.**

Outraged MPs last night demanded an immediate ban on the screening, which will unleash the most explicitly sexual language yet beamed into the nation's living rooms.

10 And the pressure will be on Home Secretary Douglas Hurd, who is proposing to set up a new watchdog Broadcasting Standards Council, to crack down on the media bosses now.

The cascade of expletives will pour out to viewers at the rate of
15 two a minute during the 45-minute show on November 4. The crudest, most offensive word is used 17 times.

The programme, a filmed recital of a poem called 'V.' written and read by Newcastle
20 poet Tony Harrison, was given the all-clear by the Independent Broadcasting Authority after it took the unusual step of showing it to the full board.

25 Originally it was to have been screened in a mid-evening slot but Channel 4 has now put it back to 11.30 p.m. 'V.', written by Harrison in
30 1985, is based on obscene grave yard graffiti and uses football hooligan slang. The title stands for 'versus' and

43

Commentary

The writers have selected emotionally loaded words to describe aspects of the poem: 'four-letter', 'filth', 'expletives', 'crudest', 'most offensive'. This generates a negative response towards the poem, though examples of the actual language used, and the context in which it is used, are not given. The reader will supply possible examples and contexts from his/her own system – for example, each reader may have his or her own candidate for 'the crudest, most offensive word', but is assumed to share the opinion of the article. The article, therefore, draws on a range of different values relating to a certain kind of language use – language that is deemed obscene – but assumes a set of shared values that the reader has no way of verifying.

This negative response to the poem is reinforced by the use of metaphor, which forces the reader to make inferences about the messages the text is carrying. The poem is described as 'a torrent of four-letter filth' and 'the cascade of expletives'. 'Torrent' and 'cascade' both give the impression of a powerful and unstoppable flow. The fact that it is a torrent of 'filth' makes the image stronger. The linking of 'filth' with fast-flowing water leads directly to images of a sewer. The article is therefore indirectly making the reader draw the inference that a TV channel is pouring sewage into people's homes, more specifically, their 'living rooms', a point that, if made directly, might be dismissed as overstatement.

The emotion required of the reader is, therefore, disgust and 'fury'.

The opposition to the broadcast apparently comes from 'the political establishment', 'outraged MPs' and 'Home Secretary Douglas Hurd'. The way in which the meaning is coded here is interesting. The use of the definite article 'the' with 'political establishment' implies a previously established group that the reader is already familiar with. This would lead the reader to assume that the Government was involved. This is reinforced by reference to 'Home Secretary Douglas Hurd'. However, the actual text makes no reference to any action or comment by the then Home Secretary, merely uses a modal verb, 'will', to imply that some related action may be requested. The phrase 'outraged MPs' apparently implies 'a lot of MPs who were outraged'. A less apparent, but probably more accurate meaning is 'those MPs who were outraged'. Later in the article, only two are mentioned.

The implication of the text is that the Government objected to the broadcast, backed by a large number of MPs, and strong action would be taken.

The subject matter of the poem is not given in the first few paragraphs of the article, but the phrase 'most explicitly sexual language' carries the implication that the subject matter of the poem will be sexually explicit. In fact (as is noted later in the article), the possibly offensive language relates to the language of graffiti and the language used by skinheads. The fact that this information is given later in the article allows the reader to generate a negative view of the broadcast before these details are given.

The readers' initial assumption may be that the subject matter of the poem is sexual.

All of these responses are generated by the use of common norms of language by which users of language negotiate meaning. In face-to-face interaction, meaning can be discussed and negotiated, the discourse can be interrupted or redirected by either or all parties involved. In the case of written text, the reader has first to identify the meanings indirectly contained within the text. Second, if the text relates to something outside the readers' immediate experience (and an as yet unbroadcast TV programme must fit this description) then the reader has no choice but to accept the information as translated through the text.

The overt role of the newspaper article is to transmit news. The analyses in the previous sections suggest that different methods of readership identification and address can be used to present information in a way that guides and directs the response of the reader by putting him/her in the role of the implied reader and creating a system of shared values that may not actually reflect the opinions of the individual members of this group. If the reader uncritically accepts the article as an item of news (and how many people read newspapers with the close critical attention that this kind of analysis requires), the implications contained within the article, and the inferences that he/she is being guided to draw from it, may be accepted at face value.

EDITORIALISING

It is easier to respond to opinion when it is open and addressed directly to the recipient as opinion rather than concealed and addressed to the recipient as fact. Editorials exist to allow the newspaper (usually in the person of its editor) to comment, give views on and draw conclusions from the day's events.

As the activity on pp. 37–38 above noted, newspapers create an implied audience by overt identification in which the paper becomes an individual and the readers are a named group – *Sun* readers or *Mirror* readers. The papers mark their editorial section in a similar way. The broadsheets (who do not, as a rule, refer directly to their readers as a group) don't mark the editorial in any specific way, apart from headlining it according to topic. The tabloids identify themselves by name, and mark the editorial specifically as opinion or comment. The exception here is the *Sun* which marks its editorial as 'The *Sun* Says', making reference, perhaps, to the spoken voice – this paper talks to its readers.

Text: Opinions

The editorial gives a newspaper the opportunity to address its readership directly, and the editorial is the place where the reader may expect to find overt comment on the news of the day. However, the 'created' reader, the implied reader, is again in evidence as the editorial addresses a group with shared (but not always explicitly expressed) values.

Text: Liberty is from the *Daily Mail*, and refers to changes in the law relating to the rights of people who have been arrested to remain silent, and the right of asylum seekers to claim financial support while their claims are going to appeal.

Text: Liberty

What a liberty

LADIES and gentlemen of the jury, consider these two facts:

Since the Home Secretary curbed the right to silence, the number of suspects refusing to answer police questions has almost halved. Likewise, the number coming here and claiming asylum has plummeted by 50 per cent since Michael Howard insisted on preventing those of them who enter the country on false pretences from living off benefit.

Both these reforms were enacted against sustained protests from self-proclaimed libertarians. And both are now getting results which should delight law-abiding Britons who prize any enlargement of their freedom from justice-cheating crooks or foreign spongers.

The headline appeals to the reader to develop a sense of indignation or outrage – 'What a liberty' is a well-known phrase for expressing indignation against someone who has been unreasonable or disrespectful. It reflects the speaking voice, an exclamation, and the writer doesn't specify whose voice this is – maybe that of the reader as implied reader, or the newspaper as narrator, championing the cause of the reader.

The speaking voice continues, but now in the context of a law court, and the reader, who is now the member of the 'jury', is addressed by the voice of the barrister. As readers, we are given two potential roles. We can be either 'self-proclaimed libertarians' or 'law-abiding Britons'. At first glance, there seems to be some equivalence between the two groups. The structures of the phrases are identical, but the meaning is not. 'Self-proclaimed' has become a term of abuse implying doubt as to the status of the self-proclaimed individual. 'Law-abiding' has more of

47

a factual status and clearly indicates a desirable quality. 'Libertarian', which means literally a believer in the freedom of the will, has become associated with groups that want to remove all legal restraints on personal behaviour, but there is no recognised libertarian movement. 'Britons', on the other hand, again has some factual status, and appeals to senses of patriotism. The implied reader is, therefore, a person who upholds the law and is a patriot. This person will listen with approving respect to the 'facts' that the voice of the barrister is giving. This is slightly different from the overt identification of a readership in the previous examples, but it does, in effect, push the reader into identifying with one group – the group that agrees with the editorial, and therefore shares the values of the paper.

The editorial then goes on to the facts of the argument. The 'facts' relate to the decreasing numbers of people who take their right to silence under police questioning, and the decreasing number of asylum seekers coming to Britain since changes in the law were made. These facts do have verifiable status as they contain figures that presumably can be checked, even if they are not precise – 'almost halved' and '50 per cent'. Both the reader and the implied reader can identify the factual status of these figures. However, towards the end of the report, these facts are extended without any signalling so that those arrested become 'justice-cheating crooks' and those claiming asylum in Britain (not just those appealing against refusals to grant asylum) become 'foreign spongers'.

The underlying implication here is that any person arrested and wishing to claim the right to silence is guilty, and any asylum seeker is here only to take advantage of the benefit system. The reader may, or may not share these views, but they are presented as having a factual status:

- They are presented in a factual context: 'the number . . . *has* almost halved'; 'the number . . . *has* plummeted'.
- They are presented as desirable: 'curbed the right to silence, insisted on preventing . . . false pretences'.
- The final move from the factual to the non-factual is embedded in a complex sentence that begins with a fact delivered in a statement: 'both *are* . . . getting results', moves to an opinion that appeals to the implied reader expressed through a modal verb: 'which *should* delight law-abiding Britons', and finally attaches the 'fact' to Britons' 'freedom from . . .'

THE SUN SAYS

Salute from the Poms

DOWN UNDER they are having the biggest and longest birthday party in history.

It is exactly 200 years since the first British fleet, with its mixed cargo of sheep stealers, pickpockets and naughty ladies, dropped anchor in Botany Bay.

However, there are skeletons at the feast.

"What is there to celebrate?" demand a thousand placards.

The Aussies are being asked to tear out their hearts over the plight of the poor old Abos.

They are asked to believe that, before the white man stole their land, Australia was a paradise inhabited by gentle, trusting, children of nature living on the fat of the land.

In fact, the Aboriginals were treacherous and brutal.

They had acquired none of the skills or the arts of civilisation.

They were nomads who in 40,000 years left no permenant settlements.

The history of mankind is made up of migrations. Australia no more belongs to them than England does to the Ancient Brits who painted themselves blue.

Left alone, the Abos would have wiped themselves out.

Certainly, they have suffered from the crimes (and the diseases) of the Europeans.

Tamed

That is inevitable when there is a collision between peoples at different stages of development.

The Aussies tamed a continent.

They have built a race of tough, bloody-minded individualists.

We have had our differences — over politics and more serious things like cricket — but when the chips were down they have always proved true friends.

Not bad at all for a bunch of ex-cons!

We hope that they enjoy their long, long shindig and crack a few tubes for the Poms.

Activity

Read Text: Salute, which appeared in the *Sun* in January 1988, about the Australian bicentenary celebrations.

◎   What shared values is the editorial trying to promote?
◎   Who is being addressed?
◎   What 'facts' is the reader being asked to accept?
◎   How does the editorial attempt to give these factual status?

Summary

Newspapers are not simply vehicles for delivering information. They present the reader with aspects of the news, and present it often in a way that intends to guide the ideological stance of the reader. The tabloids, in particular, are very clear about their own voice (THE SUN SAYS, etc.), and a lot of the time pretend that they are addressing a coherent group of people, their own readers. The *Sun* reader, the *Mirror* reader – these groups are frequently referred to, appealed to and invoked.

The broadsheets, too, identify their own readership as some kind of homogeneous group with identical aims, beliefs and opinions. The *Guardian*, for example, is happy to satirise the popular image of its readers – a strip cartoon that appeared regularly in the *Guardian* had two young financiers discussing their future in-laws as 'Guardian readers', using this term as shorthand for 'left-wing'.

The *Independent* began its advertising with the image of its reader – the person whose views and opinions are their own – with the slogan: IT IS – ARE YOU?

The problem is that these groups don't exist in the way the papers pretend. Most people have probably read the popular tabloids, and most broadsheet readers will have read rival publications even if they have a preference for one particular one.

However, the creation of groups in this way has the effect of implying the existence of a body of opinion, and frequently opinion that is associated with qualities that the majority of people who read the articles would find desirable. There is no logical reason to assume, for example, that the 'law-abiding people' of the previous *Daily Mail* editorial form a coherent group, or even an easily identifiable group (are 'law-abiding people' those who never break the law, or does this term include people who occasionally fiddle their taxes or insurance, or who sometimes exceed the speed limit when they are driving?

50

Different people will have different views), that they all support changes to the asylum laws or to the right to silence. There is probably a very wide range of views on the subject. The editorial presented, though, equates the quality of being law-abiding with a particular attitude, and leads the reader to assume that this attitude is shared by a large number of people.

Extension

1   Collect some editorials. Can you identify a 'group' that is being addressed? What language devices are being used to create and address that group?
2   Find articles that either address the reader directly, or that identify a group such as *Sun* readers or *Mirror* readers. What values are the individual reader or these groups supposed to hold? How does the newspaper establish these values?

Representations of groups: words, words, words

Writers of fiction have often speculated about the role of language in the forming and maintaining of social structures and roles. George Orwell, in his book *Nineteen Eighty-Four*, postulated a society in which the ruling powers tried to maintain almost total control over the population. A weapon in this control was the language Newspeak, which contained no way of expressing concepts and ideologies that were opposed to the state. The creators of Newspeak believed that without the language to express the concepts of rebellion, rebellion would be impossible. If people didn't have the words to formulate the concept of rebellion, the theory went, then rebellion could not happen. An example that Orwell gives is the word 'good' and its opposite 'bad'. The meanings of these words can be made more exact, and less open to individual interpretation, if the opposite of 'good' becomes 'ungood'. Degrees of 'goodness' and 'ungoodness' can be expressed by the clear and strictly defined (by the state) terms 'plusungood ', 'doubleplusungood', instead of the more vague 'more', 'very', 'rather', etc.

Modern research into language and mind suggests that people do not depend on language for thought. Babies can think before they have language, and adults frequently have the frustrating experience of not being able to find the words that exactly express the thought they had. Orwell's vision of a population controlled by its language is an unlikely, or even an impossible one. Language use is, anyway, so creative that a system that worked on the principle of one word = one meaning would not continue to do so for very long.

Even so, language can be a powerful tool. It is, perhaps, at its most powerful when its role in presenting the world to an audience is not explicit; in other words, it is easy to resist a particular viewpoint or ideology when you know it is being presented to you, but not so easy to resist when the viewpoint or ideology is concealed.

The unit on audience (Unit 3) looked at the way newspapers can artificially construct an audience (the implied audience), as a way of manipulating the actual audience into taking on a role or stance that they may not otherwise have taken. This section looks in more detail at the way language can be used to represent particular groups to promote particular attitudes or conform to an existing stereotype.

Certain groups tend to be disadvantaged within particular societies. People are defined by their sex, their race, their sexuality, their religion – and these groups can be disliked, feared, discriminated against or actively persecuted. Language is one of the means by which attitudes towards groups can be constructed, maintained – or challenged.

For example, some people have a physical disability. Their mobility, their sight, their hearing may be in some way impaired. These groups are often identified by their disability. They are 'the handicapped' as a general group – more specifically they are 'the blind', 'the deaf', 'the crippled'. This form of naming defines people by one aspect of themselves, and many are unhappy with this labelling, just as many people would be unhappy to be defined as 'the freckled', 'the big-nosed' or even 'the hearing' or 'the seeing'. Such labelling can create a situation in which people lose their individuality and become just their disability. Pressure to change this kind of labelling has encouraged society as a whole to reconsider their attitude to people with disabilities and has revealed a lot of unrecognised discrimination and unfairness. Many people with disabilities now reject the label 'disabled' and prefer the term 'differently abled'.

Newspapers are cultural artefacts. The print media of different countries and different cultures differ in a variety of ways. The American press, for example, has tabloid newspapers that are very different in format, and in many ways in content, from British tabloids. An American journalist, Randy Shilts, in his book chronicling the AIDS epidemic, *And The Band Played On*, made reference to 'the always hysterical British press'. This is not to say that the British press is necessarily worse or better than the press of other countries – but that whatever it is, it is a product of the culture it comes from.

This is an important point to bear in mind when dealing with the language of newspapers. Everything that is written in a newspaper has to be transmitted through the medium of language. The transmission of a message through language almost of necessity encodes values into the message. Language gathers its own emotional and cultural 'loading'. What this loading is will depend on the nature of the culture or sub-culture in which the language exists.

For example, if a particular culture has little respect for certain groups, concepts or beliefs, then the language for expressing ideas about those groups, concepts or beliefs will reflect that attitude. Therefore, when these things are written about, people reading the text will have their attitudes reinforced by the way the language presents these things to them. This is not to say that we are trapped by language. Beliefs and values change, and language changes as well. It does mean, however, that language can inhibit people from critically evaluating the opinions and views they hold – a fact much relied on by advertisers, politicians and all those whose function in life is to manipulate social attitudes.

Language operates at a series of levels. Written text has a visual or **graphological** level. Spoken text has an aural or **phonological** level, which, however, can also be exploited by written text. All texts have a word or **lexical** level, and all texts have a structural and grammatical or **syntactic** level. It is also important to remember that texts operate within a cultural context; that is, they are created within a particular culture, and operate within the value system of that culture. This unit looks at the way in which word choice can create an ideological slant towards groups.

A simple and obvious way in which language can be used to present specific ideas about a group is through the choice of words used to name and describe that group.

WHAT'S IN A NAME?

Naming is an aspect of language surrounded with social rules and pitfalls. In most cultures, it is possible to cause offence by adopting the wrong naming strategy towards people. In France, for example, the use of *tu* and *vous* operates to specific social constraints. An English speaker, using these forms as though they were equivalent to the English social rules for formal or casual address, is very likely to get them wrong, and cause offence.

55

Activity

Below is a list of possible forms of naming in English. For each one, try to identify a context in which one person might choose to address or name another in this way, and the relationship between the speakers implied by the name form chosen. You may find that each form carries more than one possible context and relationship. What attitudes can be implied by the naming strategy used?

Naming forms

First name only (e.g. Elizabeth, Robert); short form of first name only (e.g. Liz, Bob, Rob); first name + last name (e.g. Elizabeth Smart); title + last name (e.g. Ms, Mrs, Miss, Mr, Master); title only (e.g. Sir, Madam); last name only (e.g. Smart, Shaw); nickname (Di, Fergie); profession or trade (e.g. Doctor, Constable); formal title + name (Lord Archer, The Right Honourable John Major); formal title (Her Royal Highness, Madam Speaker, My Lord); anonymous address (boy, girl, you); assumed name – given by others (Maggie [Thatcher], The Comeback Kid); assumed name taken by the named individual (Sting, Snoop Doggie Dogg); other group (dearly beloved, comrades, ladies and gentlemen, girls, boys).

Context

Classroom, interview (job), interview (TV or radio), article, informal chat, ritual or ceremony, situation relating to profession or trade, other (specify).

Relationship to named individual(s)

Formal, informal, friends, relations, strangers, superior, inferior, colleagues, senior colleagues, other.

Commentary

Naming, context and relationship operate together to create a complex series of meanings. It is not possible in most cases to attach one meaning to one form of naming. For example, the terms 'Sir' and 'Madam' would tend to imply a formal relationship that may be mutual (Sir ÷ Sir). It isn't possible to say whether the participants know each other as this form can be used whether they do or not. These forms can also imply an imbalance (Sir or Madam ÷ first name). It can also be used in situations where the power balance is not in favour of the person addressed as 'Sir'. The police may address a member of the public as 'Sir', even though they may be planning to arrest or question that person. The use of 'boy' or 'girl' implies an adult to child relationship and, when used by one adult to another, can be deeply offensive.

The use of nicknames can indicate friendship and affection, though imposed nicknames can indicate that the namer feels that he/she has the right to impose a label on the named.

Looked at fairly simply, it is possible to generalise to a certain extent. From the point of view of the addressee, being addressed by first name only suggests either equal status or inferior status, title and last name suggests a formal situation or superior status, short form of first name suggests friendship, nicknames suggest close friendship, formal title suggests superior status, a ritual form suggests participation in a particular ritual (a court hearing, a parliamentary debate), as does specific group naming.

However, the system of naming can be manipulated to create very specific effects.

Activity

Look again at the article 'Four-Letter TV Poem Fury', discussed on pp. 44–45. This time the full article is reproduced.

- ◎ How are those opposed to the broadcast named?
- ◎ How are those in support of or associated with the broadcast named?
- ◎ Does the naming influence the attitude the reader might take to the production?

Commentary

A clear pattern emerges when the naming strategies used in this article are looked at. Those who oppose the broadcast are given their full names: 'Gerald Howarth', 'Teddy Taylor', 'Mary Whitehouse'. They are also given their titles where appropriate: 'Tory MP Gerald Howarth . . . Teddy Taylor'. They are, therefore, accorded respect in the context of the article.

Those supporting the broadcast are named differently. The poet Tony Harrison is given his full name once, and a form of title 'Newcastle

57

Text: Poem fury

FOUR-LETTER TV POEM FURY

By JOHN DEANS and GARRY JENKINS

BROADCASTERS are lining up for a head-on clash with the political establishment over a planned Channel 4 programme featuring a
5 **torrent of fourletter filth.**

Outraged MPs last night demanded an immediate ban on the screening, which will unleash the most explicitly sexual language yet beamed into the nation's living rooms.

10   And the pressure will be on Home Secretary Douglas Hurd, who is proposing to set up a new watchdog Broadcasting Standards Council, to crack down on the media bosses now.

The cascade of expletives will pour out to viewers at the rate of
15 two a minute during the 45-minute show on November 4. The crudest, most offensive word is used 17 times.

The programme, a filmed recital of a poem called 'V.' written and read by Newcastle
20 poet Tony Harrison, was given the all-clear by the Independent Broadcasting Authority after it took the unusual step of showing it to the full board.

25   Originally it was to have been screened in a mid-evening slot but Channel 4 has now put it back to 11.30 p.m.

'V.', written by Harrison in
30 1985, is based on obscene grave yard graffiti and uses football hooligan slang. The title stands for 'versus' and

when published in an antho-
logy of the poet's work it was
dedicated to miners' leader
Arthur Scargill.

Last night Tory MP Gerald
Howarth called for the programme to be withdrawn.

'This is another clear case of
the broadcasters trying to
assault the public by pushing
against the barriers of what is
acceptable, on the basis that
the more effing and blinding
they can get into everyday
programmes, the better.'

Mr Howarth, who last year
won a major legal battle with
the BBC over claims that
Fascists had infiltrated the
Tory Party, described 50-year-
old Harrison as 'another probable Bolshie poet seeking to
impose his frustrations on the
rest of us.'

Another Tory MP, Teddy
Taylor, also appealed to
Channel 4 chiefs to see sense.

'Obviously Channel 4 is the
place for experiment, and for a
bit of variety, but a poem
stuffed full of obscenities is
clearly so objectionable that it
will lead to the Government
being forced to take action it
would prefer not to have to
take,' he added.

And clean-up campaigner
Mary Whitehouse said: 'The
sooner the Government brings
broadcasting under the
obscenity laws, the better for
everyone and particularly the
public.

But 'V.' was defended by
the poet, the IBA and
Channel 4.

Harrison said: 'The lan-
guage is an integral part of the
poem. It is the language of the
football hooligan and is seen
and heard every day.'

'I don't see that it should
merit any fuss whatsoever.'

The IBA said the film had
been viewed by the board at
the request of Director-
General John Whitney.

A spokesman said: 'It was
considered very carefully,
especially given our statutory
duty as far as matters of taste
and decency are concerned.
But we came to the view that
it was acceptable.'

A Channel 4 spokesman
said: 'We stand by our decision, which was taken after
careful consideration and full
discussion with the IBA.'

But he accepted that the
film 'may be disturbing to
some', and a warning will be
given to viewers before it is
shown.

poet Tony Harrison', though this title does not recognise the fact that
Tony Harrison is an internationally respected poet. Later in the article he is
named as 'Harrison', an address that, in the context of full titles, suggests
inferior status, or at least less respect. When Gerald Howarth is mentioned
a second time, he is named as 'Mr Howarth', not 'Howarth'.

Others supporting the broadcast are anonymous: 'a spokesman', 'a
Channel 4 spokesman'. The overall effect is to reduce the status of the
supporters of the broadcast, by using naming strategies that imply that
they are either inferior or anonymous.

Naming is, therefore, a very useful device in promoting a particular
response from an audience. In the case of the article looked at in the last

activity, naming is one device used to 'slant' a text in a particular direction in relation to an issue – the broadcast of a programme – and more widely, to promote the view that certain television channels need controlling to stop them broadcasting 'obscene' or 'corrupting' material.

Another way in which naming can be used to create a particular ideology is in promoting attitudes towards particular social groups.

NAMING OF GROUPS

Within a particular culture, the rules for naming can be complex, and the selection that a particular text makes from the possible names it can give to a group can, as the analysis above suggests, be very important in transmitting ideological values to the reader of the text.

Activity

Look again at Text: Salute (p. 49). Do the names used for the three groups mentioned carry the same connotations? Do these terms give a favourable or unfavourable picture of each group?

Group	Name
Australians	Aussies, Europeans
British	Brits, Europeans
Pre-colonials	Abos, Aboriginals

Commentary

At first glance, the terms seem equivalent. The short forms ('Aussies', 'Brits', 'Abos') are nicknames that suggest an affectionate irreverence. However, in the cultural context – that of white supremacy and colonialism – the terms do not have, and cannot be used with, equivalent values.

'Aussie' and 'Brit' both name groups that have a nationality – Australian and British. 'Abo' implies statelessness. The term 'Aussie' seems to be being used within an historical context that suggests that only the descendants of the first European settlers are included within the term. Are the descendants of the people who were already there when the settlers arrived not also nationals?

'Aboriginal' is originally an adjective meaning 'first or earliest known'; or 'earlier than European colonists'. The noun 'Aborigines' came into the language as travel and colonial expansion began, used to refer both to pre-colonial groups and to animals and plants. It therefore carries strong connotations of 'primitive', 'underdeveloped' and possibly 'sub-human'. The word 'Aboriginal' gradually developed a specialised meaning that referred directly to the pre-colonial inhabitants of Australia, but by its very nature it implies that this group belongs more to other, non-specified, pre-colonial inhabitants of various countries than it does to the country its members inhabit. In other words, it is a term loaded with value judgements.

All three short forms can be used as terms of abuse. However, it is a feature within groups that terms of abuse relating to the group can be exchanged within the group (for example, it is sometimes acceptable for the term 'nigger' to be used within the Afro-Caribbean community, whereas it is completely unacceptable outside that group). In the context of the editorial, the British and the Australians belong to the same group – Europeans. In this context, the term 'Abo' then becomes a term of abuse.

The importance and significance of naming in social groups

The importance of naming can be seen in the way that oppressed or disadvantaged groups within a society try to take control of the naming strategies that that society takes towards them. This can be seen in the black community, particularly in America, where the term 'Negro', largely adopted by white Americans as the acceptable naming form, was firmly rejected by the community and terms such as 'person of colour', 'black', 'Afro-Caribbean', and 'African-American' were used in a community forced to name itself, and perhaps to avoid the unacceptable grouping of all non-whites into an apparently homogeneous group called 'coloured' or 'black'.

As the activity above suggests, naming probably becomes less important once a group achieves equal status not just in the law, but in actuality. In Australia, the pre-colonial peoples are still seriously disadvantaged. Naming matters.

Attributes, roles and qualities

The naming strategies adopted by a text can, therefore, have a direct effect on the ideological slant of the text. A further aspect of word choice is the way in which groups are described. Description can appear as part of the naming strategy – to call someone a 'man' or a 'boy' or a 'Brit' is descriptive. Description can also be added by modification in the noun phrase (p. 20) and by the use of adjectives. In the article 'Four-Letter TV Poem Fury', Tony Harrison is described as 'another *probable Bolshie* poet', the use of the modifying phrase 'probable Bolshie' adding descriptive detail that adds to the image of the poet that the writer of the article is trying to create.

Activity

Look again at Text: Salute. What descriptive detail is given about the participants? What attributes and qualities do they have?

Commentary

The Aboriginals are described as being 'treacherous and brutal'. The qualities 'gentle' and 'trusting' are mentioned as being falsely attributed to them by others. The descriptions contained in the naming compare the Aboriginals to 'children', and 'Ancient Brits who painted themselves blue'. These descriptions portray either the concept of the savage – a sub-human species; or the noble savage – a sub-human species with a child-like innocence. Both of these representations are caricatures that are rooted in early colonialism.

The white Australians, on the other hand, are 'tough' and 'bloody-minded'. They are named as 'individualists', a description that contrasts strongly with the portrayal of the Aboriginals.

Therefore, closely linked to naming are the attributes and qualities that groups or individual members of groups are credited (or discredited) with when they are discussed in newspaper texts. Newspapers are artefacts of the dominant cultural norm, as discussed in Unit 1 (Introduction). The attitudes of the dominant culture tend to be reflected in the language of news stories, particularly those about minority power groups.

REPRESENTATIONS OF WOMEN

The following articles appeared in the press in the Summer of 2001. They all have women as their central figures, but the only other criterion in the selection process was that they should not be 'glamour' items: beauty, fashion or page three texts. What words are used to refer to women in these stories? What impression does the text give in relation to the roles these women play and the qualities they have?

You might find it useful to look at:

◎   direct naming
◎   use of modifiers in noun phrases
◎   adjectival description
◎   choice of verbs to describe actions and processes attributed to these women

Women are named in the following texts in an informal or casual way – *Cherie, Ellie, Clare, Kate, Mary*. This informal naming is not exclusive to women – men are frequently named informally in newspaper articles. However, in stories relating to policy, male politicians are less likely to be referred to by their first names. For example, in the same column that the Clare Short article appears, Black Dog, men are referred to by their full names or their last names, and their roles or titles are given in full: ITN Washington correspondent James Mates, Alastair Campbell, the Prime Minister's most trusted adviser. Jeffery Archer remains Lord Archer or Archer throughout the article. Two of the women, one of whom has ministerial status and one who is a prison governor are 'bosses' (*their boss, boss of Wayland Prison*) a word that perhaps reinforces the stereotype of a woman in charge as overbearing or bossy. Ellie Barr, a woman with a lower status job, is referred to as a 'girl'.

The naming strategies adopted also refer to the women in their roles in relation to other people, particularly their families: Yvonne Ridley is a mother and three-times married, Cherie Blair is a wife, Ellie Barr is mother-of-two, Kate Cawley is single.

Adjectival description, and modification in the noun phrases focuses on the domestic lives and physical attributes of these women, even though these stories are not show-business, glamour or fashion related. The

63

Text: Women (1)

STEWARDESS SCOOPS £135.000

Spy talk raises fears for the captive mother

By **Chris Brooke**

FEARS were growing yesterday for the safety of captured British journalist Yvonne Ridley after it was revealed that she was under investigation for 'spying'.

A 'special mission' is reported to have been sent from the Afghan capital Kabul to question the 43-year-old mother, who is being held under armed guard in the eastern Afghanistan city of Jalalabad.

The developments increase concerns about the interrogation the Sunday newspaper reporter may face and the alarming possibility that she could be charged with spying by the Taliban authorities.

In convicted by a court she would face a possible death penalty.

The announcement by Kabul radio made no reference to the length of the investigation or when she may come to trial.

But with attacks by Special

Daisy: 'I miss her so much'

'She is on a big adventure'

Forces on terrorist bases in Afghanistan likely soon, the chances of her being released quickly appear to be fading.

Three-times married Miss Ridley has a daughter, Daisy, who is nine on Wednesday. She returned to her boarding school in Cumbria yesterday after spending the weekend with her grandparents Allan and Joyce Ridley at their home in County Durham.

'Daisy knows what the situation is and she is coping very well,' said Mrs Ridley, 74. 'We have told her mummy is on a big adventure. She just listens and does not show a lot of emotion.'

In a statement, Daisy, whose father was a colonel in the Palestine Liberation Organisation, said: 'I just want mummy to come home. I miss her very much and I want them to let her go. She's a very kind person and she wouldn't do any-

thing wrong.' Yvonne Ridley was arrested by the Taliban after slipping into Afghanistan illegally and without a passport. She is said by a news agency with ties to the regime to be living in a secure 'house' while the authorities check out her credentials.

According to the Afghan Islamic Press, one official said: 'She is detained not in a room but in a house and walks around in the house and in the courtyard. She is well.

'She wants to eat four or five times a day, she wants cigarettes and fresh clothes, and we are providing everything to her.'

Her mother said: 'She will probably have insisted on those things. Knowing Yvonne, she will get her own way during this. I have been wondering about how she has been getting her clothes changed, but knowing Yvonne she will be demanding things from them.'

A Foreign Office spokesman said they remained 'deeply concerned' for Miss Ridley's welfare, adding: 'There have been no new developments over the weekend, but obviously contacts are being made with officials about her situation.'

NICE LITTLE NUMBER: Mel B with ITV talent show winner Ellie Barr

Magic moment for jackpot girl Ellie and no mistake

AIR stewardess Ellie Barr scooped a £135,000 jackpot on the ITV talent show This Is My Moment after being mistakenly invited on to the programme.

Fifty contestants are usually selected to audition for the show presented by Mel B, but an error on Saturday night resulted in one extra being invited – and for mother-of-two Ellie, 51 became her lucky number. The 40-year-old who

comes from Ballymoney in County Antrim, attracted 270,769 telephone votes, each of which earned her 50p, with the song Streets of London.

Ellie said: "I think 51 is definitely my lucky number. It's the same number as my sister's house, my parents stayed in a hotel room number 51, I was contestant 51 and it's even proved lucky for England winning 5-1!"

Blair 'will quit' so Cherie can become a judge

Television documentary claims Mrs Blair will decide when her husband leaves No 10, writes **Sarah Womack**

CHERIE Blair has made a pact with her husband that he will stand down as Prime Minister after two terms to allow her to pursue her ambition of becoming a judge, a television documentary claimed last night.

Gordon Brown could even make her Lord Chancellor, if he becomes prime minister, it was said.

The suggestions were contained in a Channel 4 film, and accompanying biography, *The Real Cherie Blair*, written by Linda McDougall, the wife of another Labour MP, Austin Mitchell.

Both the Blairs have privately acknowledged the difficulties faced by Cherie in becoming a High Court judge, or law lord, while he is premier, because of accusations of cronyism and the problems of her long absences.

According to the programme, however, Mr Blair is committed to repaying his wife, who gave up her political ambitions when he landed his Sedgefield seat.

"Either way," said Miss McDougall, "Cherie will decide when Tony goes."

The film, which triggered complaints from Mrs Blair, 47, and protests by influential friends, painted a picture of a woman scarred by her parents' divorce, but determined to escape the poverty of her Liverpudlian upbringing.

Nora O'Shaughnessey, a teacher, said: "When Cherie came up to junior school, there were wonderful reports from the infant school. 'Wait till you get Cherie,' they used to say. "And sure enough, you would explain something, decimals or whatever, and in a flash she had it."

Mrs Blair left school with 4 A-grade A-levels and achieved a first at the London School of Economics before coming top in her Bar finals.

Her father Tony Booth's philandering – he had seven daughters by four women – caused her intense embarrassment and left her with an abiding hostility to the press.

It was only when she stood, unsuccessfully, for Labour that she realised the benefits of his celebrity status – he played Alf Garnett's "scouse git" son-in-law in *Till Death Us Do Part* – and asked him to help her canvass for votes.

The programme said that it was the mother of Pete Clark, her first boyfriend, who encouraged her to enter the legal profession. Mr Clark was head of a rival school debating team, and Mrs Clark, after hearing Cherie "demolish" her son, told her she would make a good lawyer.

Other revelations included that she is a dreadful driver – she had to have most of one car rebuilt – flirty, and no domestic goddess.

Her meagre beginnings have, it was claimed, made her resentful when the family sold their house in Islington for £750,000 – losing around £1 million at today's prices – when they moved into Downing Street.

Cherie and Tony Blair: he is ready to repay his wife's support

Text: Women (3)

ARCHER'S IRON LADY

Mary lookalike is governor of crook peer's new prison

By JOHN KAY and FIONA REARDON

THIS is the glamorous prison governor who will keep Lord Archer under lock and key in his new jail.

And Kate Cawley – boss of Wayland Prison in Norfolk, where the crooked peer was sent yesterday – bears a striking resemblance to his wife Mary.

Both Kate, 41, and scientist Mary 56, are high-fliers who favour a functional, businesslike look.

But beyond the straight hemlines and plain colours lies a carefully-groomed, stylish beauty.

Inmates regard single Kate as "tough but fair". She keeps trim with aerobics, horse-riding and ski-ing – and drives a sporty Mazda.

Archer was transferred to medium-security Wayland from London's Belmarsh Prison, where he was sent three weeks ago for perjury and perverting justice.

Razor

His new "home" in Thetford was where gangster Reggie Kray spent three years before he died of cancer last year.

Prison Service chiefs chose it for Archer, 61, as it is only 50 miles from his home near Cambridge, enabling his family to visit him easily.

The jail, built in 1985, has four two-storey wings surrounded by a 35ft fence topped with razor wire.

It holds 624 all-male inmates. Many are lifers and the jail runs a sex offender treatment programme.

Eight years ago it was slammed by an inspector because of "thuggery and drug-taking". One inmate had been murdered and 18 assaulted.

It has since bounced back to become a model jail. But a prison source said "Archer won't enjoy it. There are a few particularly nasty characters there and he will have to watch his back all the time."

The peer's hopes of being sent to a cushy open jail were dashed when he was classified as a Category C prisoner, due to a police probe into his money-raising activities for Kurds.

The Sun Says – Page Eight

Stylish . . . Lord Archer's wife Mary   *Resemblance . . Kate*

UNRELATED? Icelandic pop star Bjork and Clare Short

The eyes have it, Clare. . .

MANDARINS at the Department For International Development have a new nickname for their boss Clare Short. They call her 'Bjork' because of her supposed similarity to the wacky pop singer from Iceland. Which is probably where Tony Blair would like to send Short after her untimely attack on George Dubya.

domestic status and ages of Cherie Blair, Kate Cawley, Mary Archer, Ellie Barr and Yvonne Ridley are given. Kate Cawley is 'glamorous', 'bears a striking resemblance to (Archer's) wife', has 'a carefully groomed, stylish beauty'. Cherie Blair is 'scarred by her parents' divorce', is 'a dreadful driver', 'flirty', 'no domestic goddess'. Clare Short, by association, is 'wacky'.

These women perform few actions. Many of the verbs relate to their attributes. Kate Cawley 'bears a striking resemblance', she 'keeps trim'. Often, they are on the receiving end of actions. Tony Blair will stand down to 'allow' his wife an opportunity, Cherie Blair is 'scarred by her parents' divorce', her success is at the behest of others, mostly male – her husband who will 'allow' her, her father's 'celebrity status'. A woman who may have been influential in her life choices is identified via a male contact: she was 'encouraged' by 'the mother of Pete Clark, her first boyfriend'; Yvonne Ridley is 'questioned', she is 'being held', she 'could be charged'.

A random selection of stories suggests that certain stereotypes are operating in the press in relation to women. There is a tendency to depict them as existing primarily in relation to their families – their children, their husbands or partners rather than as individuals in their own right. Women are frequently described in relation to their physical appearance. Women are often depicted as weaker – they are victims, they are on the receiving end of action rather than the performers of it. If this selection is representative, then the newspaper reading public receives a series of images that depict women in a way that accords with a very limiting stereotype that tends to value women in only a narrow set of roles.

ETHNIC GROUP

As was discussed at the beginning of this unit, newspapers are cultural artefacts and will reflect the prevailing norms and mores of the culture they represent. In the section on naming above, an editorial from the *Sun* was discussed. The discussion of race in this editorial represents an attitude that would be unlikely to be expressed openly in newspapers at the current time. Attitudes to race may or may not have changed, but recognition of racism, and the acceptability of racist comment, has.

Britain is usually described as a multi-racial community and overt cultural values, and legislation, operate to work against inter-race hostility. However, there is a recognisable minority who oppose the multi-racial status of this society, and at its extreme, this group campaigns for the removal of the non-white community from this country.

Text: Riots

The heat of the night

BY ANTHONY MITCHELL

POLICE were last night braced for a summer of strife after more race riots erupted between white and Asian youths.

Concerned community leaders called for calm after violence broke out in North-west England for the second time in a month.

Just before midnight last night, tension soared again as a fire broke out in a scrap yard In Burnley, Lancashire.

Police in riot gear were quickly on the scene and stood by as firemen brought the blaze under control.

The previous two nights gangs wielding baseball bats clashed in the town as officers battled to keep them apart and terrified families ran for cover.

Marauding youths smashed and burned cars, pelted police with bricks and firebombed a pub, razing it to the ground.

Mounted police charged the gangs and sent hundreds scattering for cover on Sunday night Only four arrests were made.

Jack Berry, landlord of the wrecked Duke of York pub, said: "We were watching them smashing the windows and torching it. We were terrified. We all feared for our lives. It was quiet one minute, then the next minute there were two or three hundred Asians. They just went ballistic. We had to flee."

He and his wife have been so sickened, they are now planning to leave town.

Yesterday, as Burnley started clearing up after two nights of violence, Home Office Minister John Denham told the Commons the rioting was "deeply disturbing" and said a solution must be found at local level.

Just four weeks ago Oldham, 20 miles from Burnley, suffered Britain's worst race riots for a generation. Further "copycat" violence broke out in Bradford and Leeds.

Now there are fears that if the weather stays hot as it was on Sunday when temperatures hit the 80s, there could be clashes on the streets of many cities.

In Burnley, Chief Superintendent John Knowles said crowds taking to the streets only made the police's job harder and he urged people to stay indoors.

He said a detailed investigation was already under way with further urgent meetings between police, council and community leaders planned.

The British National Party, which polled more than 11 per cent of general election votes in Oldham, has also enjoyed some success in Burnley. It has been accused of fanning the flames of racial hatred. In the Commons, Mr Denham hit out at the "exploitation" of underlying causes by far-Right groups.

Publicly, police and community leaders claim Burnley does not have a race problem, but privately some confess it is now on a knife-edge. The trouble started on Saturday after white and Asian youths clashed at a party. Trouble spilled out on to the street and cars were smashed.

Hours later, an off-duty Asian taxi driver was attacked by white thugs who hit him with a hammer, leaving his cheekbone badly fractured. Family and friends claimed it took police over 30 minutes to come to his aid, bringing allegations of racism.

Tensions simmered for the next 24 hours and on Sunday a gang of Asians took to the town centre to vent their anger. That culminated in violent clashes.

Burnley has a population of 91,000, with 6,000 from ethnic minorities, mainly Pakistani and Bangladeshi. Deputy Mayor Rafique Malik said that Asians felt angry and vulnerable because of the time taken for police to attend the cabbie. "If police took half an hour to arrive, what faith do we have that they will protect our people?" asked Mr Malik, a retired teacher originally from Pakistan. But he added: "I have been a councillor here for 30 years and most voters are white and have always supported me. The white community is not racist, only a few individuals."

Burnley council leader Stuart Caddy said: "Everybody is pulling together to try to resolve this. We do not want to look back. We need to go forward and lessons need to be learned."

Though this group is in the minority, the way the language reflects the ethnic make-up of the community suggests that the non-white community is still seen as somehow different, possibly outside the main grouping contained within the term 'British'. In linguistics, the term **unmarked** is used to refer to a properties of language that are more general, neutral or common than a corresponding property which is said to be **marked**. The way language is used in relation to ethnicity in this country suggests that we use language in a way that is socially marked and unmarked. Thus, the term 'British' is frequently used as a term to refer to the majority community in this country, i.e. white. If non-white members of the community are included, this is often given specific reference. *Ethnic minority*, *British Asian*, *Black British* all mark this separation.

How, then, do newspapers deal with issues of ethnicity, and how are stories reported in which ethnic group is an important factor? In the summer of 2001, a series of riots erupted in the north-west of England, particularly in Bradford, Oldham and Burnley. These riots reflected an underlying racial tension that was exacerbated by the presence of extremist political groups including the National Front and the British National Party.

Activity

The article opposite appeared in the *Daily Express* on the 26 June 2001, after a weekend of rioting in Burnley, Lancashire. How are the participants named? How are they identified in noun phrases? What descriptions and attributes do they have?

Commentary

The participants are generally identified by group, rather than as individuals. *Police, white and Asian youths, community leaders, firemen, gangs, officers, terrified families, marauding youths, mounted police, crowds, police, council and community leaders, white thugs, gang of Asians, ethnic minorities, Pakistani, Bangladeshi, British National Party.*

There are a few references to individuals: *Jack Berry, landlord of the wrecked Duke of York pub, Home office minister Jack Denham, Chief Superintendent John Knowles, Deputy Mayor Rafique Malik, Mr Malik a retired teacher originally from Pakistan, Burnley council leader Stuart Caddy.* One individual is identified but not named: *An off-duty Asian taxi driver.*

It is interesting to note that where race is specified, it is more often 'Asian' than 'white'. 'White' is used where confusion may otherwise exist, for example, most of the references to the rioters refer to *'white and Asian youths'*, but occasionally the groups are identified as 'white' or 'Asian' for clarity. The ethnic minority groups are more often identified by race than clarity might require. 'Asians' are identified as 'vent(ing) their anger' and 'angry'. White groups are not similarly identified, though reference to voting patterns suggest that there is similar discontent and anger felt within this group.

When individuals are named, only the members of the ethnic minorities are identified by race: *Mr Malik a retired teacher originally from Pakistan*. Here, the paper has found it necessary to qualify Mr Malik, both by his profession and by his country of origin. Other named individuals are not identified in this way unless it is relevant to the story. The fact that the names of the individuals may indicate ethnic group does not invalidate this point. In fact, Rafiq Malik is more clearly identified as Asian by his name than Jack Berry, John Knowles, John Denham and Stuart Caddy are identified as white.

This pattern of naming suggests that being a member of the non-white community can be seen as the 'marked' form, and that when ethnic group is not identified, then the assumption of 'white' can be – and frequently is – made. Even if this meaning is not intended, it can act in a way that excludes certain groups. For example, do we assume, purely from naming, that the police and fire-fighters are white? The context offers no clarification.

Activity

One of the issues that was discussed in the papers in relation to this particular riot was whether Burnley now had serious race problems. To what extent is this discussed in the article? Look at the direct and indirect quotes in the articles. Who is quoted, what reporting verbs are used and what, if any, comment is made on the quotes?

Commentary

Indirect quotation is taken from *Home Office Minister John Denham, Chief Superintendent John Knowles, police and community leaders, family and friends* of *'an Asian taxi driver', Deputy Mayor Rafiq Malik*. The indirect quotes from the named authority figures are reported with the neutral terms 'told' and 'said'. The authority groups – police and community leaders – 'claim' and 'confess'. The verb 'claim' is often used by newspapers to make comment that cannot be substantiated or to cast doubt on statements. The doubt is exacerbated by the use of the verb 'confess'. The article, while not overtly commenting on the overall state of race relations in Burnley, does imply that there are problems.

The individuals' quotes are reported with the neutral verbs 'said' and 'asked'. However, an oblique comment is made on the words of Mr Rafiq. The second part of his utterance is reported with the clause 'But he added.' 'But' is more standardly used as a clause co-ordinator. Its use at the beginning of a sentence is a marked form that gives it emphasis. 'But' has a range of uses, one being to indicate contrast. If two concepts are in contrast, it means that one is surprising or unexpected in view of the other. The previous sentence ends with 'Mr Malik, a retired teacher originally from Pakistan.' Is his subsequent comment surprising in relation to his national origin, or in relation to his original comment? In the context, this matter is ambiguous and could be seen as a comment on Mr Malik's impartiality both as a councillor and as an observer.

Summary

Word choice is a powerful tool for establishing an ideological stance. The examples discussed in this unit show the way in which the beliefs and prejudices of a society can be reinforced by language use that supports an existing belief system. The use of belittling, demeaning or derogatory terms towards a disadvantaged group can help to promote the beliefs that the group itself is to blame for its disadvantage – the Aboriginals deserved to lose their land, women are weak and can have only a limited number of roles; ethnic minorities are dangerous and sub-human. Very few people would agree with these statements, but many would read, without challenging them, these views expressed in newspaper articles, because the views are not expressed overtly, but concealed in the word choice.

Extension

1   Look at the way members of minority power groups are named in newspapers of other cultures and countries – America or Australia, for example.
2   Identify a story that focuses on a woman. Compare the naming

71

strategies used for this woman, and the qualities and attributes she is described as having. Is there any difference between the tabloid and the broadsheet newspapers here? How do the mid-range tabloids employ naming strategies?

3   Look at the way ethnic minority groups are represented in broadsheet, tabloid and mid-range tabloid newspapers. Look at examples from ten and twenty years ago. How are naming strategies employed, and what, if any, changes have taken place over time?

Making monsters: syntax

As the previous units have suggested, newspapers frequently act, or attempt to act, as opinion formers. This section will look at some of the ways in which larger units of language can be used to define the parameters of a particular news item and to promote a dominant cultural norm. The aspects that will be looked at in some detail are **syntax**, which deals with word order, and the relationships that exist between elements in the clause.

Syntax is an important factor in the way a text creates meaning. The way in which elements within a clause are ordered can give weighting to one or more aspects, and reduce, or remove, others. The relationship between elements has a fundamental role here.

In traditional grammars, verbs are often defined as 'doing words', that is, as actions. Anyone who has tried to label word classes using this definition will have found that it is not really very helpful, as the following sentences demonstrate. The verbs are highlighted.

1   (Mary) Bell **pays** the price
2   One question **remains**
3   Their freedom **could cost** the taxpayer £5 million
4   They **are** pure evil
5   People **found** the sentence unacceptable
6   They **went** on holiday

Some of these verbs could be described as actions – *went, could cost, pays* – but the others don't really fit that definition. *Remains, are, found,* refer more to states and processes.

A useful way of looking at syntax is to consider the participants and the relationships between them, between the processes represented by the verb, between concepts of place, time and manner. What elements are essential parts of the structure, and what are optional? Where have optional elements been used, and what role do they play in the creation of meaning or the relationship between narrator and narratee?

Some of the verbs above establish a relationship between participants (people, emotions, places, concepts): A person and a sum of money, the cost to the taxpayer of freeing people, the response to a sentencing decision.

In other cases, only one participant is involved in the process. 'They', 'One question'.

The following analysis gives a model of the verb system that is useful for identifying ideological functions in texts:

- ◎ Verbs that require two participants: an actor and something that is affected by the action: Bell (actor), pays (action) the price (affected). These verbs take a **direct object** or are **monotransitive**.
- ◎ Verbs that operate with one participant: One question (subject) remains. These verbs are **intransitive**.
- ◎ Verbs that require three participants, an actor, a directly affected and an indirectly affected. Their freedom (actor) could cost (action) the taxpayer (indirectly affected) £5 million (affected). These verbs take a direct and an **indirect object** and are **ditransitive**.
- ◎ Verbs that require an equation between actor and a quality or a person or an object. They (actor) are (verb) pure evil (quality of actor). Another example of this kind of structure is They (actor) remain (verb) the most notorious killers in the country (quality of actor). These verbs are **intensive**.
- ◎ Verbs that take a complement like monotransitive verbs, ie they take a direct object. The direct object then takes a complement in the same way that intensive verbs do. For example, People (actor) found (action) the sentence (direct object) unacceptable (quality of direct object)

Another model of the verb system can also be useful for identifying ideological functions in texts. Verbs can be divided into two kind, those that refer to actions – **actionals** – and those that refer to relations – **relationals**. Actional verbs can be divided into those that have an agent or actor who causes the action, and someone or something that is affected by the action (as, for example, in sentences 2 and 3 above).

These verbs are called **transactives**. The other actional verbs – *went* – involves only the actor. There is no identifiable person or thing affected by the action. Verbs like this are called **non-transactives**.

$$
\text{actional} \left\{
\begin{array}{l}
\text{transactive} \\[1em]
\text{non-transactive}
\end{array}
\right.
$$

Relational verbs can either represent the relationship between someone or something and a quality or attribute (as in sentence 4 above), or indicate an equal state between two nouns (as in sentences 5).

$$
\text{relational} \left\{
\begin{array}{l}
\text{quality or attribute} \\[1em]
\text{equal state}
\end{array}
\right.
$$

It is important to recognise that *transactive* and *non-transactive* don't mean the same as *transitive* and *intransitive*. To be transactive, a verb must represent an action that goes from the actor to the affected, as in *Mary Bell pays the price*. The label *transitive* is applied to any verb that takes a direct object, so *He swam the river* has a transitive structure, but it is not transactive. No process goes from the actor to the affected. Transactive structures can be converted into passive forms (for a discussion of passives see page 83 below). *The river was swum by him* is an awkward construction in English.

By selecting from the range of models, the producer of text can present the world to the reader with an ideological slant imposed upon it. Are people or regimes presented as actors or recipients of action? Are they presented in terms of their behaviour or their qualities? This next section will look at some of the ways selection from the verb system can affect the ideological stance of the text.

MAKING MONSTERS: MARY BELL, JON VENABLES AND ROBERT THOMPSON

Child murder is, sadly, an aspect of human behaviour in all cultures. The majority of child murders occur within the family group. Some – a very small number – are carried out by strangers. A rarity is the deliberate murder of one child by another. It would be hard to dispute that a consensus exists which sees child murder as one of the most reprehensible crimes that can be committed, and newspaper reporting of these crimes reflect the seriousness with which our culture views them.

However, as with all news items, editorial selection can operate to decide which stories are given a high newspaper profile, and the focus of the profile that is given. Some people convicted of child killing attract the interest of newspapers long after their conviction.

The names of Ian Brady, Myra Hindley, Rose West, Fred West, Mary Bell, Jon Venables, Robert Thompson are probably recognised by the majority of the adult population.

Some are gradually forgotten. The names of Marie Therese Kouao, Carl Manning and Robert Oliver are less well known, even though the crimes they committed against children were horrific.

Others still are given status as victims or – possibly – heroes.

In 1997, Louise Woodward was convicted in the US of the murder of a baby, Matthew Eapen, who had been in her care. There was an outcry in this country, and at least two of the tabloid newspapers led campaigns for her release. The conviction was later reduced to manslaughter by the judge and Louise Woodward was freed.

In 1993, two ten year old boys were convicted of the murder of a toddler, James Bulger. They were tried in an adult court, and their names were released to the press. There was an outcry against what was seen as lenient sentencing particularly in the tabloid press. In 2001, the decision was made to release them from custody.

Both stories have aspects in common: Both cases attracted much campaigning attention from the British press, supportive to Louise Woodward, deeply hostile towards Jon Venables and Robert Thompson, they both relate to people convicted of child murder, they both relate to cases that were problematic and controversial: several newspapers in this country depicted Woodard as a victim of a miscarriage of justice from the start of the trial because of her youth and inexperience. Though Thompson and Venables were only ten years old when they committed their crime, much of the reporting of their case saw them as fully responsible and fully culpable.

Activity

Look at the following headlines that appeared after the news of these releases broke:

Set 1: Louise Woodward

1   'A compassionate conclusion' (*Guardian*)
2   Freed! (*Mirror*)
3   Free (*Sun*)
4   Mercy (*Daily Mail*)

Set 2: Jon Venables and Robert Thompson

5   Freed (*Daily Mail*)
6   Bulger's Mum weeps as Bulger's murderers go free (*Daily Express*)
7   Bulger boys go on hols (*Sun*)
8   Coming to a street near you (*Daily Star*)

Which of these headlines contains a verb? Can you classify these according to the categories identified on page 74 above? Who are the participants? What qualities are attributed? What effects are created?

Commentary

Of the set 1 headlines, one contains a word that could be a verb, but is given no syntactic context. No other verbs are used.

Three of the headlines in set 2 contain verbs, and one contains a word that could be a verb but is given no syntactic context.

The set 2 headlines contain one intransitive form, *weeps*, one intensive form *go* (free) and two prepositional forms, *go* (on hols) and *coming*.

The set 1 headlines contain no actors. The focus is on the state or condition of Louise Woodward, or on the quality of the judgement that has been made.

The set 2 headlines contain the actors *Bulger's mum*, *Bulger's murderers* and *Bulger boys*. James Bulger's mother is present as an actor whose actions have no recipient or affected participant. Her action is intransitive: she weeps. Jon Venables and Robert Thompson have qualities: they are *free*; and the headline also gives them location: they are going on holiday. Headline 8 contains an implied actor, Thompson and Venables; and a location that contains an implied threat directed at the reader: *near you*. The effect, therefore, is to arouse emotions: anger at the contrasted states of the boys and the mother: *weeps*, *go free* resentment at the implied privilege given to the boys: *on hols*. (The abbreviated form also carries a note of frivolity which may enhance the sense of resentment); fear at the threat of proximity. The use of intertextuality (see Unit 2 above) in headline 8 carries the same effect of frivolity. The implication is that Thompson and Venables, or those charged with their care, are not taking these events seriously.

Activity

The following texts appeared in the *Sun*, November 11 1997, the date when Louise Woodward was released and January 9th 2001, the date when Jon Venables and Robert Thompson were granted anonymity by the courts in preparation for their eventual release.

◎ How are actional and relational verbs used in relation to Louise Woodward, Robert Thompson and Jon Venables?
◎ What actions are performed by each?
◎ What qualities are attributed to them?
◎ What other participants appear in the stories?

Text: Monsters?

FREE

Louise is out of jail...but must stay in States

From BILL COLES in Cambridge, Massachusetts

OVERJOYED Louise Woodward was free last night after a judge dramatically ruled she could leave a U.S. jail.

The British nanny, 19, looked numb with shock as Judge Hiller Zobel sentenced her to 279 days, the time she has already spent in prison.

Louise must stay in the States pending an appeal. But her release brought ecstatic scenes at home.

Hours earlier, Judge Zobel reduced her conviction for murdering baby Matthew Eappen to manslaughter at

Continued on Page Two

JUSTICE FOR LOUISE

Moment of truth . . . Louise in court last night as she hears her fate from judge Hiller Zobel   Picture: Sky TV

Nanny set free

Continued from Page One
the court in Cambridge, Massachusetts.

It was an incredible turnaround for the teenager, coming just 11 days after she was given life with a minimum of 15 years.

The news had relatives and pals back at Louise's local pub The Rigger in Elton, Cheshire, jumping into the air and screaming for joy.

Announcing the new sentence, Judge Zobel said it was "time to bring the judicial part of this extraordinary matter to a compassionate conclusion."

Louise was told she cannot leave the state or apply for a passport to leave the States until a prosecution's appeal against the verdict is heard.

Her defence lawyer Barry Scheck also pledged to appeal to clear her name completely.

HUGGED

Judge Zobel asked Louise if she had any questions to ask him. She replied: "No, thank you, your honour."

Louise had been held in high-security Framingham Jail since she was first arrested for killing Matthew in Boston last February.

In court, a dozen of her friends and family smiled and hugged each other as the judge announced the new sentence.

Her parents Gary and Sue broke into a grin

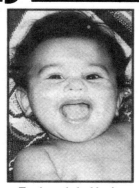

Tragic . . . baby Matthew

for the first time since the case began.

Matthew's parents Debbie and Sunil were not in court. A friend said they had gone away after receiving a barrage of hate mail.

Louise calmly maintained her innocence when she was given the chance to speak to the court while waiting to hear her fate.

She stood up and declared: "I say what I said at my last sentencing — I am innocent."

Wearing a smart blue jacket, Louise appeared relaxed, showing little sign of the emotion that erupted when the jury found her guilty.

Louise's lawyer Andrew Good told the hearing, shown live on Sky TV: "The defendant does maintain her innocence and that is a matter of her constitutional right."

He also urged Judge Zobel to use his common sense when determining sentence. He said: "I am sure the

court will use appropriate discretion."

State prosecutor Gerard Leone had called for Louise to get at least 15 years.

He told the judge: "The defendant has not acknowledged doing anything wrong which would equate to manslaughter."

Louise faced an anxious wait while the court was in a brief recess as Judge Zobel considered the submissions of both sides.

She sat stony-faced with her legal team, occasionally exchanging a few nervous words.

After the hearing lawyer Mr Scheck described the whole case as "very tragic."

COURAGE

He sympathised with the Eappen family for Matthew's death but added: "We have great respect for the courage the judge showed."

Judge Zobel's decision comes after a huge campaign to free Louise, which included a £33,000 fighting fund from Sun readers.

Jean Jones, who has led the campaign for Louise in her home village of Elton, said: "Deep down I know this will not have damaged her too much.

"She will still be the Louise Woodward we know and love.

"When she gets off that plane the first thing she will want to do is sit down and have a gossip."

The Sun Says — Page Eight

Text: Monsters?

LUXURY LIFE OF BULGER KILLERS

Treats, trips and gifts for pair

By JOHN TROUP and GUY PATRICK

THE boy killers of James Bulger have led an amazing life of luxury since being caged, The Sun can reveal.

A whopping £1.6million has been lavished on Robert Thompson and Jon Venables — who yesterday won the right to slip back into society anonymously.

Taxpayers have footed the bill for plush rooms with **VIDEOS** and **TRIPS** to the seaside — as

Continued on Page Four

Thompson . . . own video

Venables . . . plush room

James . . . killed by pair

80

Text: Monsters?

LIFE OF LUXURY

'Disgusted' .. Ralph Bulger

Mum Denise .. 'slap in face'

Continued from Page One well as for the finest **EDUCATION** money can buy. Judge Dame Elizabeth Butler-Sloss yesterday ruled the 18-year-olds — just ten when they kidnapped and murdered toddler James — must be released in secret.

She said: "I am compelled to take steps in the almost unique circumstances of this case to protect their lives and physical wellbeing."

Lawyers for Thompson and Venables claimed the pair — set for parole early this year — feared revenge attacks.

But the ruling was a snub to The Sun and other newspapers who argued the move would mean hated killers like Myra Hindley could insist on being freed in secret.

James's mother Denise, 33, stormed: "The judge has slapped me in the face.

INJUSTICE

"Whatever corner I have turned, I have been faced with injustice." Ex-husband Ralph, 34, said: "I am disgusted."

Their son was just two when Thompson and Venables snatched him from a shopping centre in Bootle, Merseyside. They tortured him to death for kicks — and left his body on a rail line. The crime shocked the nation but the killers have served just eight years in separate secure units.

And they have had the kind of privileged upbringing — including private one-to-one tuition — their poverty-stricken families could only have dreamed of.

Former truant Thompson has passed five GCSEs and is studying for his A-levels.

Last night a spokeswoman for the victim support group Mothers Against Murder and Aggression said: "It is an utter scandal."

Commentary

Louise Woodward is the subject and actor of relational verbs: *Louise Woodward was free, The British nanny looked numb with shock, Louise appeared relaxed*; the past participle *overjoyed* is placed in a prominent position as modifier of the proper noun Louise Woodward. The reader therefore focuses on her qualities. She is also the subject of non-transactive actionals, *(the time) she has spent in prison, Louise must stay in the states, she cannot apply for a passport, She stood up, she sat*.

There are very few transactive structures in which she is the actor. Those that there are relate to abstractions — there is nothing physical affected by her actions: *Louise calmly maintained her innocence, Louise faced an anxious wait, the defendant does maintain her innocence, the defendant has not acknowledged doing anything wrong*.

Where she is a participant in transactive structures, she is frequently the affected: *Judge Hiller Zobel sentenced her to 279 days, Judge Zobel reduced her conviction, Judge Zobel asked Louise, when the jury found her guilty*.

Several of the sentences in which she is the subject are passive structures. These will be discussed below.

Interestingly, the only sentence in which she is equated with the quality of guilt is a complex transitive *when the jury found her guilty* in which the attribution of guilt is ascribed to a third party.

Other participants in this article are the judge, the prosecuting and defending teams, Louise Woodward's parents, the victim, the parents of the victim, a family friend, and readers of the *Sun* newspaper. The victim appears three times, twice as the object of a non-finite verb and once as a possessive modifier. His parents appear once in relation to their absence and as the recipients of hate mail. The majority of the participants have a direct involvement with the case with the possible exception of *Sun* readers and the family friend.

Thompson and Venables appear as participants in a high percentage of the sentences in article 2. The majority of these are transactives in which they, or one or the other of them, is the actor: *The boy killers of James Bulger have led a life of amazing luxury, who yesterday won the right, the pair feared revenge attacks, Thompson and Venables snatched him, they tortured him to death, (they) left his body on a rail line, the killers have served just eight years, they have had the kind of privileged upbringing their poverty-stricken families could only have dreamed of, Former truant Thompson has passed five GCSEs.*

Non-transactive actionals are in the minority. *(he) is studying for his A-Levels*

Many of the transactives focus on the crime that the two boys committed, others relate to the levels of privilege the boys are seen to have had while in custody. The privileges are enumerated: videos and trips to the seaside.

Other participants are the victim, taxpayers, the judge, lawyers, Myra Hindley, the victim's parents, Thompson and Venables families, a spokeswoman for Mothers Against Murders and Aggression, and the *Sun* newspaper. The victim appears as the object of transactive verbs. His parents are quoted extensively. Thompson and Venables' parents are not directly mentioned – just 'families' who are ascribed the quality of being 'poverty stricken'. Many of the participants have no direct involvement with the case, though their inclusion may equate them with the case in the readers' minds: taxpayers, Mothers Against Murder and Aggression, and Myra Hindley.

The two cases as presented by the *Sun*, make an interesting contrast. Louise Woodward is presented in terms of her qualities, her options and as the recipient of other people's actions. Jon Venables and Robert Thompson are presented in terms of their actions or of 'privileges' of which they are the recipients.

DELETING THE ACTOR

In the example above, the relationship between actor, process and affected is looked at. The choice of a transactive structure can focus the attention of the reader on the actor, and present a particular picture of an individual or group. In the above examples, Thompson and Venables are frequently subjects of a trasactional verb, which places emphasis on their participation. Louise Woodward, on the other hand, is more frequently the subject of non-transactive actionals and relational verbs which allows the reader to focus on her qualities and attributes.

A different effect may be created if the actor is either placed in a less prominent position in the clause, or removed altogether.

In the section above (p. 74) different types of verb were looked at. One of these was monotransitive verbs, verbs which can take a direct object.

English has the capacity to allow the rearrangement of **transitive** clauses so that the **direct object** of a verb becomes the subject. For example, the clause

(subject)	(verb)	(direct object)
The dog	bit	the postman

can be written as:

(subject)	(verb)	(adjunct)
The postman	was bitten	by the dog

The second structure, *the postman was bitten by the dog* has the effect of putting more emphasis on the person or thing affected by the action and less on the actor, but also allows for the actor to be removed from the clause altogether:

The postman was bitten

Structures such as *The dog bit the postman* are called **active**, or said to be in the **active voice**. Structures such as *The postman was bitten by the dog* are said to be **passive** or in the **passive voice**.

Activity

Look at the articles from pp. 78–81 again.

- ◎ Identify any passive structures.
- ◎ What effect do they create?

Commentary

The passive structures in these article are:

Article 1

1 . . . *coming just 11 days after **she was given life** with a minimum of 15 years.*
2 ***Louise was told** she cannot leave . . .*
3 ***Louise had been held** in high security Framingham jail since **she was first arrested** . . .*

Article 2

1 . . . ***since being caged.***
2 ***A whopping £1.6 million has been lavished** on Robert Thompson and Jon Venables.*

The first passive structure in article 1 does not occur until paragraph five. The article is structured to focus on Louise Woodward by placing her in subject position, but at the start, she is the subject of relational verbs that give her qualities that attract a sympathetic response. In each case, the actor is deleted from the passive structures, thus taking away reference to many of the legal authorities that prosecuted Louise: the judge who sentenced her, the police who arrested her and the authorities who held her in prison. These become anonymous, possibly reducing the force of the original charges against her.

In article 2, only two passive structures are used. The first one allows the use of the word *caged* in relation to the two boys. This gives them the quality of animals. There is no actor – we are not told who caged them so no one is directly implicated in having done this. The second passive places them in relation to *taxpayers money*. The deletion of the actor places the two boys in the structure as 'quasi-actors'. They are the recipients of benefits but the deletion of the actor allows the implication that they are also the actors.

Summary

The cases of Louise Woodward and Jon Venables and Robert Thompson became the focus of major news campaigns. Both cases were highly controversial and raise important social issues: the wisdom of entrusting children to young, inexperienced and underpaid adults, the scandalously under-regulated American au-pair system; the culpability of immature, emotionally and behaviourally disturbed children, the capacity of the legal systems of the two countries to deal with the ambiguities of these cases, the justifications of treating ten-year-olds as adults for the purposes of the legal system. Neither of these articles address these issues. They adopt straightforward campaigning tones. Louise Woodward is a victim to be sympathised with, Jon Venables and Robert Thompson are monsters who have been rewarded for committing a terrible crime. These depictions detract from the serious news issues and turn these tragedies of both individuals and of our society into 'stories'.

MARY BELL

Mary Bell was convicted of the murder of two boys aged three and four, at the age of eleven. Contemporary newspaper reports of the trial and verdict were restrained by current standards. The *Sun*, for example, turned down Mary Bell's life story that was offered to them by her parents during the trial. Mary Bell was released in 1980 with a new identity, and protected from media intrusion by an injunction that protected the anonymity of her daughter. However, in 1998, Gitta Sereny published an account of the Mary Bell case, *Cries Unheard*. Mary Bell collaborated with her on the book, and Sereny gave Bell an undisclosed sum of money for her assistance. The newspapers, particularly the tabloids, were extremely hostile to this. Mary Bell and her family were, for a while, forced to leave their home and go into hiding because of the intrusions of the news media.

Theme

The discussion above on the articles about Jon Venables, Robert Thompson and Louise Woodward discussed the way in which the relationship between the actor and the verb could be manipulated to create a particular emphasis or focus. One of the ways in which this

85

was done was by the use of passive structures that bring to the front of the sentence something that would not otherwise have been there. The **unmarked**, or expected order of clause elements is **subject**, **verb**, **object** or **complement** and **adjunct**.

So far in this discussion of syntax, the analysis has focused on the structure of the clause. Another useful analytical tool is theme, the way in which the relative importance of the subject matter is identified. In English, the first major constituent of a sentence is the theme of the sentence, and though this is often the grammatical subject, there is no necessary correspondence between theme and grammatical element. A further device available to the narrator is the use of 'it' as a dummy subject. The use of 'it' as clause theme serves to select the subject for special attention and is a useful device for creating emphasis.

Activity

The following article appeared in the *Daily Express* on 30th April 1998.

- ◉ Does the sentence begin with the Subject of the clause, or with another clause element?
- ◉ What is the effect of deviating from the unmarked order?
- ◉ How does this affect the depiction of Mary Bell?

The pictures that accompany this article are worth a moment's consideration. As noted in unit 2 above, the combination of image and word can create meaning beyond that conveyed by either one separately. The pictures show a chronological development of Mary Bell from an appealing child to an adult concealed behind dark glasses. She progresses through the stages of *child*, *precocious*, *sullen* and *tasting adult freedom* as her move from childhood into adulthood removes the protection of youth.

The first sentence of the article focuses on this element of conceal-ment: 'After years of anonymity', 'The cloak and dagger operation'. The focus on time: 'At 1.30am' adds to this impression of something secret and clandestine. Word choice in these opening paragraphs contribute to this effect: Mary Bell is 'reduced to crouching in the darkness' she is 'bundled into' a back seat.

As a participant in these events, Mary Bell, though the recipient of actions rather than the actor, is the subject of a series of passive clauses that make her (and her daughter) the theme of the relevant clause: 'they were bundled'.

The article also focuses, via theme, on the money allegedly paid to Mary Bell. This is marked in the use of 'it' as dummy subject: '(since) it became known she received £50,000', 'it emerged Bell recently paid for a £43,000 three-bedroomed home'.

Theme is used to emphasis the impartiality of one of the people who is against this payment. 'A friend of Sereny's, he . . .'; and Mary Bell's culpabilty, 'That Bell's attempt at mitigation has been spectacularly derailed . . .'

The role of the press in revealing the whereabouts of Mary Bell and her daughter is minimised. In the only sentence in which they are named as the pursuers who have driven a woman out of her home, they are placed after a subordinate clause acting as an adverbial, *After news leaked of the payment, the press traced Bell to an address on the south coast.* Thus their presence is subordinate to the leaking of the news. (The matter of who leaked the news in the first place is not touched upon.)

The overall effect of the article is to present a picture of a woman who is the author of her own misfortune, who runs away from the consequences of her actions and who is culpable not just in the eyes of the newspaper but in the eyes of the world.

FACTS AND POSSIBILITIES

Newspaper articles are ostensibly news stories – they report information. Editorials comment, speculate and give opinion. There is a third kind of article, however, the feature article, that falls between the two. The feature article picks up an item of news, and develops it via comment, opinion and speculation.

The text on p. 89 is an article that appeared in the *Daily Mail* when the news of Gitta Sereny's book came out. It purports to be an expert opinion of Mary Bell's motives in assisting Gitta Sereny in writing her book. Given that the book was not published (other than some serialised excerpts) when the article was written, and given that Mary Bell was not available for interview, where has the writer obtained the information on which to base his article? On close reading, it becomes apparent that this text gives very little factual material directly. It gives some information about the original case, but the main part of the content is opinion and speculation.

Text: Bell

Bell can run but can't hide

BY GERARD GREAVES

AFTER years of anonymity, Mary Bell and her 14-year-old daughter were reduced to crouching in the darkness of their new home on Tuesday night as they waited for a police escort to remove them.

At 1.30am, a police Vauxhall Senator drew up alongside the end-of-terrace Victorian house and they were bundled into the back seat and driven away.

The cloak-and-dagger operation neatly summed up Bell's dramatic change in fortunes over the last week since it became known she received £50,000 for collaborating with author Gitta Sereny. The payment prompted two questions. How did a person supposedly remorseful for killing two children think she would get away with taking a considerable slice of a book advance? And how did she and the author think it would affect Bell's daughter, whose anonymity is protected by a court injunction?

In Newcastle, Bryan Roycroft, former head of social services, was legally responsible for Bell both before and during the trial.

A friend of Sereny's, he nevertheless said yesterday: "I stand entirely against her being paid. It has broken Mary Bell's anonymity by outraging people and bringing her and her child into the public eye. Gitta was ill-advised to hand over money, and Mary was ill-advised to receive it."

Her anonymity is certainly strained. After news leaked of the payment, the press traced Bell to an address on the south coast.

From there it emerged Bell recently paid for a £43,000 three-bedroom home and moved in two weeks ago. Local gossip, once long dead, is now fast catching up on the pair. As one neighbour said: "She seemed a very nice lady. She always gave a cheery hello and was a very pleasant girl. But now we know."

Indeed, from now on Bell and her daughter may be forced to run from place to place — but no one can say it is not by Bell's own doing.

Sereny yesterday denied paying Bell £50,000, but declined to name the price. She said Bell deserved the cash because she had "devoted herself" to helping with the project.

That Mary Bell's attempt at mitigation has been spectacularly derailed by the acceptance of money is now unarguable. Only one question now remains — for Bell and her daughter, what will be the final bill for the case for the defence?

OUT ON LICENCE: Tasting adult freedom

JAIL SNAP: Mary as a sullen 20-year-old

GROWING UP IN PRISON: Precocious at 16

FACE OF A KILLER: Mary as a child

THE MANIPULATOR

Why I, as a psychiatrist, believe the double child killer is using this author

By Doctor Raj Persaud
CONSULTANT PSYCHIATRIST

MARY BELL'S outpourings appear to be a common rationalisation that disturbed criminals make to try and justify their actions.

Although they claim to reveal all, they are a classic way of failing to take responsibility. And for someone as manipulative as Bell her choice of medium – journalist Gitta Sereny – is a perfect means of getting her own way.

Her decision to unburden herself to Sereny rather than to a professional clinician as part of her search to uncover her severe psychological problems is a strong hint that true understanding might not really be on her agenda.

The first hint that anyone needs when embarking on a painful exploration of themselves is privacy, which is the last thing they will get from a massively hyped book accompanied by a newspaper serialisation.

June Richardson, the mother of one of the victims, is rightly sceptical about the whole undertaking.

It is doubtful that a truly objective exercise which tackles the complex psychology of Bell can be carried out by anyone other than a properly qualified expert, such as a psychologist or psychiatrist. Indeed in all her time Bell has never sought the help of a psychiatrist.

The second hint that Bell is orchestrating her own PR is the way she passes blame for her heinous crimes on to someone else.

She puts the blame on her prostitute mother and claims she was sexually abused by her clients. But since her mother died three years ago this ensures the one person who might corroborate her story is unable to confirm or deny it.

Psychiatrists are nowadays so concerned about the dangers of patients using 'false memories' of sexual abuse that the medical Royal Colleges have issued guidelines urging extreme caution in taking such claims as the truth.

They are aware that some disturbed individuals falsely blame serious sexual assault for their problems.

Such allegations elicit sympa-

Manipulative desires and skill: Mary Bell, shown playing the recorder, in a 1973 photograph

thy and divert attention away from the issue of personal responsibility for a crime.

As sex is a taboo subject, the lay listener is manipulated into not asking too many questions about what actually happened, for fear of appearing intrusive. Sereny, however, places great emphasis on the fact that Bell told her the same allegations three times, was overwrought when she related them and showed her scars beneath her dress. In fact none of these features count for very much as proof that she is telling the full truth.

Instead, an experienced clinician would lay greater store on the details of the allegations that Bell might recall. it is precisely here that her account becomes most vague, she cannot even give a rough approxima-

tion of how often the abuse occurred. She sidesteps the question of exactly what form it took, and instead prefers to hint, allowing our imaginations to do the rest.

The question is never tackled about why at her original trial the medical examination found no evidence of sexual abuse.

Sereny gets so caught up in the emotions of Bell's claims that in the extracts so far published she does not pursue the connection between these alleged events and the two murders.

Many people are tragically sexually abused. But this does not turn them into murderers. What is missing so far is any discussion of Bell's well-known long history of violence to other children before she committed the murders. The sexual abuse

allegations have succeeded in diverting attention away from areas Bell might find truly uncomfortable to explore.

But we may never learn the connection between her past and her crimes, because she has chosen to speak to someone who cannot question her properly to ascertain the real truth.

During her examination by the four psychiatrists between her arrest and her trial, she was generally unco-operative. One of them commented later that he had seen a lot of psychopathic children, but had never met one as intelligent, manipulative or as dangerous as Bell.

Teachers who knew Bell described her as an inveterate liar who always sought attention – the precise combination of personality features which is found in those who might make

up or exaggerate stories about sexual abuse.

She was also described during the court case as having an astonishing ability to turn whatever witnesses said to her own advantage. For example, when it was disclosed that fibres from her dress had been found on a victim, she explained how she had pushed him on a swing the morning before he was killed. She had previously denied playing wiht him that day, but now, giving a swing was not the same thing as playing.

BUT the most pressing reason why Bell's claims should be subject to careful scrutiny is that she has a habit of making false claims of sexual abuse.

In the autumn of 1970 one of the male teachers at her approved school was brought to trial following allegations by Bell that he had indecently assaulted her. After her testimony, the judge directed the jury to acquit since it was clear the accusations were a fabrication. She got petulant at being questioned probingly in the witness box.

Three months earlier Bell had plotted to accuse another teacher of assaulting her. That such a prosecution was ever brought attests to the continuing depth of her manipulative desires and skill, two years after being in care and away from her supposedly culpable mother.

Sereny, in her first book on Mary Bell, wondered why the girl's accusation against her teacher got to court. She asked: 'Is this not a classic manipulation of an emotionally deprived girl? And might it not have been treated with more scepticism at the outset?'

It might be a grave pity that Sereny has not followed her own advice because Bell certainly knows how to gain attention through deception.

DELETING THE ACTION

The discussion about Thompson, Venables and Woodward above looked at the way in which people involved in the story were said to have certain attributes or emotions, such as, for example, shock or innocence. These were presented to the reader through relational verbs. Sometimes, however, a writer can present a quality or attribute in the modifier of a noun group. Is there any difference in meaning between the following sets of texts? The highlighted sections in the first pair are noun phrases taken from the article you just read, **The Manipulator**; the second pair present the information contained in the noun phrases via a clause with a relational verb.

Set 1

◎ **Someone as manipulative as Bell**.
◎ Mary Bell's outpourings appear to be a common rationalisation that **disturbed criminals** make.

Set 2

◎ Mary Bell is manipulative.
◎ Mary Bell is a disturbed criminal.

Commentary

When an opinion is given via a clause with a relational verb, it is easier to recognise that an opinion has been offered. You might have responded to the sentences in set 2 by agreeing with them or disagreeing, or even witholding agreement or disagreement on the grounds that you have insufficient information to form an opinion. The texts in set 1, however, don't alert the reader to the fact that an opinion has been offered. The writer of the article has offered the view that *Bell* is *manipulative*; and that she is a *disturbed criminal*. The way this view is offered, however, conceals the fact that this is nothing more than opinion. There is, there-fore, a difference in meaning between the texts in set 1 and the texts in set 2. Set 1 texts appear to refer to an accepted state of affairs, while set 2 texts offer an opinion that is open for discussion. By removing the relational verb, the writer can influence the opinion and ideological stance of the reader.

MODALITY

Modality refers to the way in which a text can express attitudes towards a situation, and is usually realised in the use of modal verbs (can, will, shall, may, must, could, would, should, might); and in the use of adverbs such as *possibly, likely*.

Modal verbs carry a range of meanings, and it is a mistake to try to identify a fixed one-to-one relationship between verb and meaning; as is true of most aspects of language, context is vital to meaning. An important point to remember is that any action or process that is attached to a modal auxiliary has not necessarily happened. Look at the following examples:

> He will go, he might go, he could have gone, he must go, he would have gone.

In each case there is a degree of uncertainty about the status of the verb *go*. It has either not yet been performed and may not be, was not performed, or the fact of its performance is a matter of doubt. *Will* is used in English as one way of expressing the future (English does not have an actual future tense form for the verb), and as such can have the force of prediction – this is likely to happen. *Might*, on the other hand, tends to imply that there is a strong possibility that the action or event won't, or didn't take place (he might go, he might have gone)

Activity

Read **The Manipulator** again. Identify the modal verbs and the adverbs. What degree of probability do these suggest to you as a reader?

Commentary

The modal auxiliaries in this article express a range of probabilities – *is a strong hint that true understanding **might** not be on her agenda; (privacy) which is the last thing they **will** get; it is doubtful that a truly objective exercise **can** be carried out; the one person who **might** corroborate her story is unable to confirm or deny it, we **may** never learn, an experienced clinician **would** lay greater store*

The modal verbs *might* and *can* express tentative possibility, something that is possible but unlikely: this choice implies doubt that any objective assessment of Mary Bell is possible, and doubt that her mother would have confirmed her story. The use of *might* in the first example is interesting. It expresses tentative possibility, but the possibility is reinforced by the word 'strong', and the use of the negative enhances the force of the sentence. The writer is able to cast major doubts on Mary Bell's veracity and motivation without expressing this as a fact.

The effect of scepticism and doubt is enhanced by the use of adverbs and adverbials. *Although, falsely, actually, however, in fact, instead, it is doubtful.* Many of the adverbials used are **sentence adverbials**, that is, adverbial words, phrases or clauses that convey the speaker's comment on what he or she is saying.

The use of modal verbs, and the choice of adverbs allows the writer to present opinion and speculation about Mary Bell in a way that gives it almost the status of fact.

Activity

Read the text again, and answer the following questions:

- ◎ How does the article interact with the reader? You might want to look at direct address, the use of title and status, the ordering and linking of information, the expression of opinion and assumptions of shared views.
- ◎ Does this affect the ideological stance of the text?

Commentary

The writer does not use direct address – there is no use of *you*, or even *Daily Mail readers*. There is also no named implied audience – no *law-abiding people*. There is, though, a group being referred to that the reader might be expected to identify with – *anyone, themselves, many people, them*. There is also a *we*, an unidentified group who wish to learn about a connection between the childhood experiences and the childhood crimes of an adult who has lived as a law abiding member of the community for years.

The status of the author is reinforced in several ways: he is *a psychiatrist*, a *consultant psychiatrist*. He refers to groups of experts within his clinical field: *psychiatrists, medical Royal Colleges, experienced clinician*. All such references add weight to the expertise that the writer apparently brings to the case. None of these expert opinions are actually made about

Mary Bell, or the Mary Bell case, but the reader might be guided, by the context, into assuming that there is a direct link.

The context of a clinical environment is reinforced by the implication that Mary Bell sought out Gitta Sereny: *Mary Bell's outpourings, her decision to unburden herself, Bell is orchestrating her own PR*, which is not the case.

The word choice throughout the article is designed to cast doubt on the statements of Mary Bell as reported by Gitta Sereny: *outpourings, appear to be, claim, claims* and factual status on the writer's own views and those of experts whose views were not expressed in relation to this case: *they are a classic way of failing to take responsibility, her choice of medium . . . is a perfect means of getting her own way, the mother of one of the victims is rightly sceptical, Bell has never sought the help of a psychiatrist, psychiatrists are nowadays so concerned.*

Information is presented in a way that suggests it is linked. Paragraphs 1–8 relate largely to Mary Bell and her apparent reasons for agreeing to talk to Gitta Sereny. Paragraphs 9–11 discuss general concerns in the world of psychiatry of false claims of sexual abuse, paragraphs 12–15 discuss Gitta Sereny's apparent lack of skill in the area of interviewing the victim of such abuse and her alleged gullibility, paragraphs 16–17 links false claims of sexual abuse with Mary Bell's motivations, paragraphs 18–20 describe Mary Bell at the time of her trial, paragraphs 21–24 look at false claims of abuse Mary Bell made as a child in custody.

The article addresses the reader from the stance of expert, and reinforces the views contained within the article with those of other experts. The reader is therefore asked to accept this piece as coming from an experienced clinician in this field. However, closer reading of the article demonstrates that the writer has had no contact with Mary Bell, and has only read extracts from the book. The experts quoted have made no comment on or reference to the case of Mary Bell. Despite this, the reader is being asked to accept a range of unsupported opinions that are being presented via language that is strongly emotionally loaded.

Summary

There are a range of choices that a writer can make at the level of syntax that can evoke different responses in the reader. The ones looked at in this unit are not the only ones available to the writer, but they are some of the most commonly used: selection from the verb system; relation between actor and action, including the use of passive structures; the reorganisation of clause units to make different elements of the clause the theme of the sentence; modality; and the presentation of opinion as expertise.

Note

1   The model of actional and relational verbs given in this chapter is a simplified version of the one given in Hodge and Kress, 1979, pp 8–9.

Extension

1   Analyse a selection of news reports and feature articles that you think present an ideologically biased representation of an item of news. Do news reports and feature articles use the same language devices, or is there an identifiable difference?

2   Collect news reports, editorials and feature articles that relate to the same story from one newspaper. How is the ideological stance of the paper maintained across this range?

3   Compare a similar collection across a range of newspapers. How are different ideological stances represented and maintained?

Discourse

Texts form coherent units of language that are constructed to operate in units larger than the single sentence or utterance. This section will look at the way newspaper texts form a coherent whole, carrying a clear ideological stance throughout an article. The previous units have looked at aspects of lexis – the vocabulary choices that a writer makes, and aspects of syntax, and the way these levels of language can operate in newspaper texts. Lexical and syntactic patterns are an important aspect of discourse – for example, the patterns of word choice identified in the articles in unit 4, and the patterns of modality identified in the article about Mary Bell (p. 89) help to make the text form a coherent unit.

Texts have been selected in the previous two units because they demonstrate the way in which specific groups are represented in the language of newspapers. This section will look further at representations of a group that is foregrounded because of political and social changes which have led to migrations from the poorer and more unstable parts of the world to the wealthier and more secure west.

THE BARBARIAN AT THE GATES: BRITAIN UNDER SIEGE

In the 1990s, issues of immigration, racism, racial unrest were matters of important debate. The increase in refugee numbers meant that immigration control – always a controversial topic – became a major political issue. Britain had a clear duty under various United Nation charters, to give asylum to people who were in real danger of political or religious oppression, and to offer temporary shelter to refugees. There was, however, a lot of hostility towards refugees, particularly those from groups that were ethnically in the minority in Britain. Evidence suggested that there were large numbers of people coming into Britain illegally, but also that many people with bona fide claims of refugee status were being excluded. At this time of a major clamp down on refugees, many of whom were highly educated and skilled people, Britain was actively recruiting in other countries for teachers, nurses and scientists because of serious shortages of people with these skills. There were, therefore, clear ideological contradictions relating to the status of refugees, and there were issues that demanded serious and informed debate. This section looks at the way these issues were depicted in the newspapers at the time.

IDENTIFYING PATTERNS IN TEXT

Activity

The following texts consist of two articles that appeared in the *Daily Telegraph* and the *Daily Mail* on 3 September 2001. The articles are presented separately, but the sentences in each one are presented in random order. They report an attempt by refugees in France to travel illegally to England via the channel tunnel trains. The article from the *Daily Mail* is incomplete. Only the first eleven paragraphs are used. The original texts can be found at the end of this unit, pp. 103–4.

- ◎ What language features helped you to put the texts into the correct order?
- ◎ If you reconstructed the texts wrongly, what language features misled you?
- ◎ What differences can you find between the texts in their attitude to these events, and to the people attempting to enter Britain?

1   Howling and cheering they massed at the top of the railway embankment.

2   They swarmed easily over rolls of barbed wire and a 10ft fence before emerging on the rails, triumphant.

3   This was the remarkable scene at the French mouth of the Channel Tunnel at the weekend as 100 asylum seekers made the most determined bid yet to breach security.

4   Then they hit the tracks half a mile from the entrance to the tunnel, unperturbed by a Eurostar passenger train heading past towards the promised land at 50mph.

5   Then, with rocks picked from the trackside they directed their fury at another train emerging from the tunnel, loaded with cars and their passengers.

6   Suddenly, one of the group doubled back.

7   Or more accurately, all over for the night.

8   As it became clear to the would-be illegal immigrants that their way forward was blocked, the mass advance finished almost as quickly as it began.

9   Spotting a camera crew filming the invasion from a nearby bridge, he unleashed a volley of stones from a slingshot.

10   It was all over.

11   At the mouth of the tunnel, where staff had been forced to switch off the 25,000 volt overhead cables, a freight train came to rest, blocking one of the two rail entrances.

12   Hopelessly outnumbered, a handful of security guards in fluorescent yellw jackets could do nothing but watch.

13   They launched themselves in wave after wave against the puny obstacles set in their path, hell-bent on reaching the Chunnel and Britain beyond.

Text 2

14 None of the 80 asylum seekers on Thursday night managed to get into the tunnels.

15 The would-be asylum seekers were rounded up by security staff and returned to the Red Cross centre at Sangratte.

16 Eighty illegal immigrants tried to force their way into the Channel Tunnel site in France on Thursday night in an attempt to smuggle themselves into Britain.

17 'We have increased the number of staff patrolling the portal, but if you strengthen security at one part it moves the problem elsewhere.'

18 The latest incident comes after 44 people were found earlier this week walking through the Channel Tunnel towards England.

19 Eurotunnel, which employs 300 security staff, said it had increased security patrols at the portals to the tunnels.

20 The area was already covered by CCTV and infra-red cameras.

21 'This is why a comprehensive system needs to be put in place by Eurotunnel.'

22 Kevin Charles, spokesman for Eurotunnel, said: "It's the same problem night after night, which is why the British and French governments have dumped the problem on our doorstep.

23 'Our immigration officers search vehicles on the French side of the tunnel, but it is after these checks that people get into the shuttles.'

24 'We could build a 30ft wall and they would still come back night after night.'

25 A Home Office spokesman said Eurotunnel's Coquelles terminal was still not secure and the company must do more work to combat illegal immigrants.

26 She said: 'The UK government is doing everything it can to help Eurotunnel.

27 'The bottom line is that these people will not go away.'

Commentary

You will probably find that you reconstructed the original texts without too many mistakes. The reason for this is that each text has distinctive patterns running through it that help the reader to identify a specific text, and the way the material within each text is sequenced.

LEXICAL COHESION

One of the patterns you will have identified and used is the pattern that exist within the words and phrases of a text. This is called **lexical cohesion**. Some of the patterns that exist within the texts are:

Semantic field (the use of words and phrases from a particular area of meaning.)

> The *Daily Mail* article uses a high number of words from the semantic field of conflict: massed, breach, hell-bent, hit, fury, shocked, outnumbered.
> The *Telegraph* uses very few: force, conflict.
> The *Daily Mail* uses words relating to animal behaviour: howling, swarmed
> The *Telegraph* uses the language of security, politics and law: patrols, portals, CCTV, Home Office spokesman, British and French governments.

Direct repetition (the same word repeated)

> The *Daily Mail*: massed . . . . mass, railway . . . rails . . . rail . . . , rocks . . . rocks
> The *Telegraph*: The Channel Tunnel . . . the Channel Tunnel . . . the tunnels . . . the tunnels, Eurotunnel . . . Eurotunnel . . . Eurotunnel, security . . . security . . . secure

Synonyms (words with very similar meanings)

> The *Daily Mail*: railway, rails, track, trackside; rocks, stones; mouth of the tunnel, entrances
> The *Telegraph*: illegal immigrants, would-be asylum seekers; security staff, security patrols

99

Specific to general reference (where the same thing is referred to, but the first reference has more detail)

> The *Daily Mail*: 100 asylum seekers, they
> The *Telegraph*: Eighty illegal immigrants, themselves; the Channel Tunnel site, the tunnels; the portals to the tunnels, the area, the portal.

Specific to more specific reference:

> The *Daily Mail*: 100 asylum seekers, one of the group

Level of formality (texts can use different levels of formality to address a specific topic.)

> Less formal (the *Daily Mail*): high use of metaphor and narrative structure: then . . . then . . . suddenly . . . as
> More formal (the *Telegraph*): low use of metaphor, non-narrative structure, use of official comment.

The patterns of word choice in the text carry a clear ideological message. The *Daily Mail* represents the incident as a battle in which one group of combatants almost defeats the other by overwhelming them, by violence and by animal-like behaviour. The *Telegraph* makes no reference to violent behaviour and reports the incident as a relatively minor example of current problems faced by Eurotunnel which was dealt with successfully.

GRAMMATICAL COHESION

This unit has already discussed briefly some of the patterns of grammatical cohesion that occurred in texts used in the previous unit – patterns of modality for example. This section will identify some other patterns of grammatical cohesion that will have helped you to identify and reconstruct the texts in this activity.

Activity

Look at the use of pronouns to refer to the participants in these events. In each article:

◎ Which participants are referred to by the use of pronouns?
◎ Is there any difference in the references within each article?
◎ Is there any difference between the two articles?

Commentary

The *Daily Mail* has a high use of pronouns in reference to the asylum seekers. The first reference is cataphoric, that is, makes reference forward: they ... 100 asylum seekers. This device is more commonly found in literary or persuasive language where it can create emphasis or a sense of anticipation. The persistent use of 'they' serves to anonymise these people, an effect enhanced by the use of animal metaphor. There is almost no other pronoun use.

The *Telegraph* uses very few pronouns: illegal immigrants ... themselves; Eurotunnel ... it ... we; a spokesman ... she.

Definiteness

This refers to the use of determiners. New information is frequently signalled by the use of the indefinite article *a*, information already held by the reader is signalled by the definite article *the*. The *Daily Mail* makes almost exclusive use of definite forms in relation to the asylum seekers and their actions: the storming of the chunnel, the railway embankment, the remarkable scene, the most determined bid yet. The first naming of the asylum seekers uses the post-determiner, a numeral, which emphasises the number of asylum seekers. Where new information is signalled, it relates to the trains and a security fence: a 10ft fence, a Eurostar passenger train.

The *Telegraph* also uses a majority of definite forms. The first reference to the asylum seekers uses a post-determiner (note the factual discrepancy between 100 and 80), but there is no previous cataphoric reference. The attempt on the channel tunnel is signalled as new information: an attempt.

101

Reference outside the text: exophoric reference

All the information contained in the use of pronouns and articles is contained within the text – though the *Daily Mail*'s consistent use of the definite form implies a shared knowledge with the reader that may not actually exist. This reference helps to create the implied reader who is addressed by this text. (see unit 2)

Another form of exophoric reference that occurs in these texts occurs in the use of **deictic** reference. Deictic reference is context bound – it requires information that is already in the text, or that is shared by the reader or that is available outside of the text. The use of cataphoric 'they' in the *Daily Mail* article again carries the implication of shared knowledge with an implied reader that may well not exist in the actual reader.

The *Telegraph* uses almost no exophoric reference, apart from use of the definite form referred to above.

Links between sentences: conjunctions

Sentences frequently refer back to the previous sentence or forward to the next when an argument or discussion is being developed. The *Daily Mail* uses time sequencing to link the sentences: they launched . . . they swarmed . . . before emerging . . . then they hit . . . then . . . they directed . . . suddenly . . . he unleashed . . . as it became clear . . .

The opening sentence of the *Daily Mail* article sets a dramatic scene, the context of which is obscure. The use of the deictic 'this' at the beginning of the following sentence serves to create a link forward and back.

The sentences are also linked by the establishing of a structural pattern which is then varied to place emphasis on specific structures (see theme p. 85): they massed . . . they launched . . . they swarmed . . . they hit . . . they directed . . .

The *Telegraph* creates links by time reference: on Thursday night, the latest incident, earlier this week and specific to general reference.

Summary

The patterns of lexical and grammatical cohesion identified in these texts not only help them to form complete, coherent units, but also allow the ideological approaches of the texts to develop coherently. The *Daily Mail* adopts a hostile approach towards the asylum seekers that is enhanced by its patterns of narrative sequencing, its use of

80 migrants try to enter tunnel site
(Filed: 01/09/2001)

Eighty illegal immigrants tried to force their way into the Channel tunnel site in France on Thursday night in an attempt to smuggle themselves into Britain.

The would-be asylum seekers were rounded up by security staff and returned to the Red Cross centre at Sangatte. The latest incident comes after 44 people were found earlier this week walking through the Channel Tunnel towards England.

None of the 80 asylum seekers on Thursday night managed to get into the tunnels. Eurotunnel, which employs 300 security staff, said it had increased security patrols at the portals to the tunnels.

The area was already covered by CCTV and infra-red cameras. Kevin Charles, spokesman for Eurotunnel, said: "It's the same problem night after night, which is why the British and French governments have dumped the problem on our doorstep.

"We have increased the number of staff patrolling the portal but if you strengthen security at one part it moves the problem elsewhere. The bottom line is that these people will not go away.

"We could build a 30ft wall and they would still come back night after night." A Home Office spokesman said Eurotunnel's Coquelles terminal was still not secure and the company must do more work to combat illegal immigrants.

She said: The UK Government is doing everything it can to help Eurotunnel. Our immigration officers search vehicles on the French side of the tunnel, but it is after these checks that people get into the Shuttles.

"This is why a comprehensive system needs to be put in place by Eurotunnel."

- ► 25 August 2001: Vast majority of asylum seekers beat expulsion
- ► 22 August 2001: Eurotunnel asks court to shut Calais refugee HQ
- ► 11 August 2001: Transport firms attack £12m fines for 'illegals'
- ► 4 August 2001: Asylum seekers found under Eurostar train
- ► 20 February 2001: Sangatte: the waiting room for England

Text: Migrants

The storming of the Chunnel

By Tom Rawstorne

HOWLING and cheering, they massed at the top of the railway embankment.

This was the remarkable scene at the French mouth of the Channel Tunnel at the weekend as 100 asylum seekers made the most determined bid yet to breach security.

They launched themselves in wave after wave against the puny obstacles set in their path, hell-bent on reaching the Chunnel and Britain beyond.

They swarmed easily over rolls of barbed wire and a 10ft. fence before emerging on the rails, triumphant.

Then they hit the tracks half a mile from the entrance to the tunnel, unperturbed by a Eurostar passenger train heading past towards the promised land at 50mph.

Then, with rocks picked from the trackside they directed their fury at another train emerging from the tunnel, loaded with cars and their passengers.

From point-blank range the clunk of rocks hitting the cab's bodywork rang out. Visibly shocked, the driver sped on to safety.

Suddenly, one of the group doubled back. Spotting a camera crew filming the invasion from a nearby bridge, he unleashed a volley of stones from a slingshot. Hopelessly outnumbered, a handful of security guards in fluorescent yellow jackets could do nothing but watch.

At the mouth of the tunnel, where staff had been forced to switch off the 25,000volt overhead cables, a freight train came to rest, blocking one of the two rail entrances.

As it became clear to the would-be illegal immigrants that their way forward was blocked, the mass advance finished almost as quickly as it had begun.

It was all over. Or more accurately, all over for the night.

In what has become a nightly event, rather than being arrested the migrants were offered a lift by French authorities back to where they came from.

Not to Iraq, Iran, or Afghanistan, but to the Red Cross centre at Sangatte, two miles from the terminal at Coquelles.

On Saturday not all those stopped at the tunnel wanted to go back to Sangatte.

Some casually turned down offers of lifts, slipping away into the shadows and the bushes from where they would no doubt launch another 'escape' bid.

Others climbed aboard waiting minibuses and within minutes had been whisked to Sangatte.

Back at the terminal, as usual, it was left to Eurotunnel to pick up the

'We know police can do nothing'

pieces. After the power switch-off at 10pm, the tunnel was closed for two hours.

Thousands returning to Britain before the start of the school term suffered delays of up to three hours, while freight services were cancelled overnight.

It also left tunnel security chiefs struggling to work out how to tackle the asylum-seekers' new tactics.

Although last Wednesday 44 of them managed to walk seven miles into the tunnel before being caught, the full-frontal assault on Saturday night may have been a well-planned diversion.

By tying down security staff and halting services, other immigrants hiding within the vast site had the perfect opportunity to slip on to trains.

'Everyone knew the tunnel was going to be attacked,' said an Iraqi immigrant who took part but refused to give his name.

'If we are many, then it takes many police to stop us and if we go on the track then they have to stop the trains.

'We know the police can do nothing to us but it takes them a long time to bring us back to Sangatte while others can take a chance to get on the trains.'

In broad daylight earlier on Saturday there was clear evidence of smaller groups of two or three immigrants sneaking into the terminal.

Shortly after 3pm two men carrying plastic bags containing spare clothing could be seen penetrating fencing at a remote part of the site.

Once inside they lay in tall grass beside the track waiting for nightfall and the chance to climb on board passing trains.

At 10pm they would have had the perfect opportunity as their 100 'colleagues' went over the top.

Four asylum seekers who smuggled themselves into Britain on a Eurostar train yesterday are believed to have endured a perilous journey clinging to the train between carriages as it sped through the Chunnel.

Three of the men were caught as the train stopped at Ashford International railway station in Kent, but the fourth ran off.

The three were taken to a detention centre in Dover.

It is not known at this stage where the stowaways, all Afghans, climbed on board.

The Eurostar train left Paris at 8.10am, arriving at Ashford – its first stop in Britain – two hours later, before travelling on to London Waterloo.

In wave after wave, they kept coming

Immigration officers found 40 refugees, including an eight-year-old boy, hiding in a van stopped at Dover yesterday.

When they removed the cargo of furniture in the German-registered vehicle, they found 39 Sri Lankans and one Indian huddled in a cramped hidden compartment.

Eurostar faces a fine of £2,000 for every illegal immigrant found on its trains.

t.rawstorne@dailymail.co.uk

terms relating to battle, its use of animal imagery and its appeal to shared knowledge and the implication of danger or threat averted in the development of the story as a series of threatening actions: they massed . . . they launched . . . they swarmed . . . they hit . . . they directed . . .

The *Telegraph* adopts a more formal, low key approach. It uses less metaphoric language, and has reference to official comment.

PRAGMATICS: LANGUAGE IN CONTEXT

This book has been discussing the ways in which newspapers create meaning and communicate that meaning to the reader. An important aspect of meaning is the context in which the language occurs. In conversation, an utterance such as 'It's cold in here' can carry a range of meanings. Structurally, it is a statement, a form often used to convey information. Semantically, it offers information about the temperature of a place. However, its meaning can often depend on the context in which it occurs.

Activity

What, in your opinion, is the meaning of 'It's cold in here' in the following exchanges and contexts:

Person A comes into a room and leaves the door open.
B: It's cold in here.

A: Shall I bring the coffee through?
B: It's cold in here.

A: Do you want the window open?
B: It's cold in here.

Commentary

In each case, B's response could be seen as irrelevant, but most users of English would have no trouble in understanding the responses as: *Shut the door*, *Let's have our coffee somewhere else*, *Don't open the window*.

Pragmatically, therefore, depending on the context, an utterance such as *It's cold in here* can have a range of apparently unrelated meanings that speakers usually have no problems interpreting.

A key aspect of pragmatic meaning is that of shared context, and pragmatic analysis is usually applied to spoken language. However, as has been discussed previously, newspapers often engage the reader in a form of dialogue. The implied reader is involved in a context that the newspaper assumes, and it is easy for the actual reader to also assume this context, which does not, in fact, exist. This allows newspaper language to carry meaning at the pragmatic level. In this section, two types of pragmatic meaning will be discussed: presupposition and implicature.

105

PRESUPPOSITION

A powerful tool for conveying meaning is the way in which language can assume a particular meaning without directly asserting it. For example, an utterance such as 'Have you stopped stealing cars?' contains the assumption that the addressee was stealing cars in the first place. A similar thing occurs in utterances such as 'Where did he find the car?' (Assumption – he found the car), 'What's his problem?' (Assumption – he has a problem). These assumptions that are 'built in' to an utterance, rather than directly stated, are called **presuppositions**. Certain linguistic structures trigger presuppositions: implicative verbs such as *manage* and *forget*, and change of state verbs such as *stop, begin, continue*: 'He managed to stop in time' presupposes that he stopped; 'He forgot to buy the milk' presupposes that he intended buying milk; definites and possesives: 'He could keep a car in the shed' does not presuppose the existence of the car, but 'He could keep **his/the** car in the shed' does; wh-questions: 'When did he buy the car?' presupposes that he bought the car. Competent language user will make the presuppositions that are built into and triggered by these constructions.

These presupposed meanings, as they are not directly asserted, may be accepted without challenge, particularly in the context of a newspaper article where the assumed shared context does not exist.

Activity

The following texts are taken from the article about Mary Bell (p. 87 above) and the article about illegal immigrants (p. 104)

- ◎ What presuppositions are contained in the texts?
- ◎ How may these affect the attitude of the reader to Mary Bell or to the asylum seekers?

1 How did a person supposedly remorseful for killing two children think she would get away with taking a considerable slice of a book advance?
2 No one can say it is not by Bell's own doing.
3 The storming of the Chunnel.
4 . . . they directed their fury at another train
5 We know the police can do nothing.

Commentary

Text 1 presupposes that Mary Bell believed she would get away with something, and also that she received a large advance for her contribution to the book. Text 2 presupposes the events of the article are Mary Bell's responsibility, text 3 presupposes that the tunnel was stormed, i.e. attacked, text 4 presupposes that the emotion motivating the behaviour of the asylum seekers was fury and text 5 presupposes that the police are helpless.

These presuppositions direct the reader towards a particular interpretation of the events reported: that Mary Bell is the author of her own misfortunes, and that the asylum seekers are dangerous and our defences are weak.

IMPLICATURE

Look again at the different meanings contained in the utterance 'It's cold in here' above. In each case, the listener would have interpreted the utterance differently, or drawn a different **implicature**.

Implicatures are meanings that are dependant on the context of the utterance and the shared knowledge between narrator and narratee. In conversation, speakers co-operate to achieve a shared meaning. In newspapers, as has been noted above, this sharing cannot literally take place, but the assumption that it does can be used to create meaning beyond the 'literal' meaning contained within the text.

The philosopher Paul Grice proposed a set of basic principles of conversation that speakers adhered to that make conversation 'co-operative': **the co-operative principle**. He provided an account of how it is possible in conversation to mean more than is actually said.

Grice's principles, or 'maxims':

1   Maxim of quantity: Make you contribution as informative as is required for the current purposes of this exchange. Do not make your contribution more informative than is necessary.
2   Maxim of quality: Do not say what you believe to be false. Do not say that for which you lack adequate evidence
3   Maxim of relevance: Be relevant
4   Maxim of manner: Avoid obscurity of expression, avoid ambiguity.

Grice suggests that meaning can be created when these maxims are not observed. When they are openly flouted, the recipient assumes that the co-operative principle is being adhered to, and draws implicature from the flouting of the maxim. For example, in the following exchanges:

a   Are you coming to the party tonight?
b   I'm working tomorrow.

c   This video isn't working.
d   Have you tried plugging it in?

The maxims of relevance and quantity have been flouted, but in each case, implicature can be drawn: *b*'s response in apparently irrelevant, but *a* will understand this contribution as *b* saying she is not going to the party. In the second exchange, *d*'s contribution flouts the maxim of quantity – *c* doesn't need to be told that the video needs plugging in to work. However, the implicature is contained in the response that firstly *c* has neglected to plug the machine in and secondly that *c* has made a foolish mistake.

Activity

Read the following extract from an article that appeared in the *Daily Mail*. Identify the maxims that have been flouted in the highlighted sections of text, and decide what implicature can be derived from the text.

How an author would have us believe that the killer is the real victim of the story

The role of Bell's mother is particularly expanded. Miss Sereny is convinced that **it was the death of her mother** (and not the offer of cash) which persuaded Bell to co-operate with the book.

A sensitivity for the feelings of her mother, with whom the killer clearly had a complicated relationship, was what previously prevented Bell from talking, **we are told. Now she can no longer respond,** her daughter is portrayed as more of a victim than ever before. . . . Miss Sereny accuses Betty of gross physical and sexual abuse of her daughter.

Commentary

The text appears to be flouting the maxim of quantity. We are told that Mary Bell's mother is dead. Later, we are told that she can now no longer respond. This gives the reader more information than is necessary – if Mary

Bell's mother is now dead, clearly she can no longer respond. The implicature throws doubt on Mary Bell's claim that she was abused by her mother.

The addition of 'we are told' to the previous sentence also carries this implicature. It flouts the maxim of relevance and the maxim of quantity – the reader has already been informed that the text is giving an account of the book. This again carries an implicature that casts doubt on the status of Mary Bell's story.

Summary

This unit has looked at some of the devices that operate to make newspaper texts coherent and cohesive. These devices: patterns of word choice, patterns of syntax operate to make the text a complete unit at the level of structure and at the level of meaning. Patterns of word choice and syntax can carry an ideological slant through a text, establish a relationship with the audience; and establish the nature of that audience, in the sense that newspapers often address an implied audience rather than an actual one.

The address to an implied audience allows the newspaper text to communicate with the reader at a level more often found in spoken language, using the concept of a shared context that does not, in fact, exist. The newspaper text becomes a conversation between individuals who have a shared – and therefore unchallenged – value system.

Perhaps the most important role of the reader is to recognise this creation of meaning, and be prepared to overtly accept or reject it.

Extension

1   This unit has looked at the cohesive devices in a limited range of newspaper texts. Do all newspapers follow similar patterns? Do a comparison of stories across different types of newspaper – broadsheet and tabloid; local and national are two possible comparisons – and see if these papers use the same devices to construct and maintain a particular type of discourse.

2   Can you identify attempts to address an implied audience that allow the newspaper text to use features of shared context? Is this a feature of broadsheet as well as tabloid journalism?

3   The following text is an editorial from the American newspaper *USA Today*. Does this text use the language devices identified through this book to create an ideological stance?

109

When everyone gets an A, grades are meaningless

OUR VIEW **High school seniors applying for college find that an A average isn't what it used to be.**

An A average no longer makes the grade in college placements. Just ask high school "honor" students.

Rather than heading to elite colleges, some academic all-stars are collecting rejection slips. The reason: more A-average students than ever before applying to college.

Studies by UCLA — where high school seniors with 4.3 grade-point averages often are rejected — show that 31.5% of college freshmen nationwide last fall reported average grades of A- or higher. That's up from 22.6% in 1990 and twice the level 30 years ago. Only one-fourth of college applicants average less than a B, down from 35% in 1990 and 45% in 1966.

Are today's college-bound students that much brighter or harder working than their predecessors?

Obviously not. College entrance exams aren't improving. For A students entering college, SAT scores have actually dropped several points in the past decade.

What's going on is not improved scholarship but rather inflated grading.

A U.S. Department of Education study found A's and B's in many urban schools are no better than C's and D's. Districts pump up grades for non-academic achievements, from class attendance to community service. And more than half of all school districts now weight grades, awarding bonus points for taking college prep classes.

The goal of such weighting is laudable: to reward kids for tackling tougher courses.

But the bonus-point systems differ wildly. Atlanta uses a 6-point scale. Other districts, a 5. Still others simply add a half point. And there's no consistency from district to district on which courses qualify.

Because this mishmash makes GPAs almost meaningless to college admissions offices, many are putting more weight on college admissions tests, like the SAT.

Those tests, though, give an edge to students with access to special classes on how to take them. Worse, results come too late for students or their parents to do much to improve skills to succeed in college.

Already, more than a quarter of college entrants need tutoring or remedial courses in math, one in eight in English. Catching up wastes time and money. Many college students now take a year longer to finish college than 20 years ago. And that extra year can cost an average of $7,000 at a public college, $18,000 at a private school.

What's the answer?

Some schools ditch grades altogether, relying on teacher evaluations and portfolios of students' work. But college admissions officers say portfolios soon become a blur, and evaluations must be translated into grades to compare with other applicants.

Admissions officers prefer a nationally standardized system for weighting grades. But getting all schools to agree on a standard would be difficult if not impossible.

A different approach with promise is under way at the University of Washington. Each year, grades of its students are compared with their high school records. The differences between high school GPAs and college GPAs are published each fall, giving both parents and students an assessment of their high school's grading system.

Another remedy allows students to take tougher courses to earn class honors but gives them no extra grade points. Most college admissions offices already weight grades for advanced courses on their own, so students who take on the challenge would lose no advantage in college admissions.

High school grades should mean what they say. That's the best way to give students and parents an accurate picture of what's possible in college.

Earning college credit

According to the College Board, more than 200,000 high school grads this year will start college with credits earned in high school, which can add to grade confusion. Percentage of schools participating in the advanced placement program compared with 1987:

	% in '96	Change from '87
Alabama	45	7
Alaska	12	-3
Arizona	57	11
Arkansas	27	14
California	69	15
Colorado	50	15
Connecticut	84	25
Delaware	46	-4
Dist. of Columbia	100	61
Florida	57	9
Georgia	59	25
Hawaii	68	20
Idaho	39	16
Illinois	50	22
Indiana	55	22
Iowa	29	20
Kansas	24	13
Kentucky	62	31
Louisiana	24	10
Maine	58	19
Maryland	71	10
Massachusetts	80	28
Michigan	52	17
Minnesota	44	26
Mississippi	38	26
Missouri	26	14
Montana	31	17
Nebraska	19	8
Nevada	56	20
New Hampshire	68	17
New Jersey	85	26
New Mexico	42	24
New York	72	18
North Carolina	64	23
North Dakota	7	5
Ohio	58	20
Oklahoma	16	7
Oregon	44	9
Pennsylvania	60	20
Rhode Island	74	25
South Carolina	70	20
South Dakota	14	10
Tennessee	50	20
Texas	51	31
Utah	70	10
Vermont	66	24
Virginia	70	16
Washington	53	10
West Virginia	63	44
Wisconsin	57	40
Wyoming	30	17
Total U.S.	52	19

Newspapers on-line

With the advent of new technology, many newspapers now provide an online presence. These are informative in varying degrees. Some provide a minimal presence and some reference to current newspaper content, some provide a wide range of resources. The following list identifies a few of these. Given the changing nature of the internet, this information is not intended to be exhaustive.

The *Guardian* and *Observer*
www.guardian.co.uk

The Guardian Unlimited site is a useful and wide ranging resource. It offers current news, breaking news, features, issues, wide ranging talkboards (though these can be a bit cliquey), audio, picture, resource lists, live interviews and an archive from 1998. A very useful online presence.

The *Telegraph*
www.telegraph.co.uk

This site offers current news, breaking news, features and issues and an archive facility going back to 1994. The archive is limited for earlier material, but useful for later.

The *Independent*
www.independent.co.uk

Current news, breaking news, features, issues and an archive facility going back to 1999. Links to Independent digital sites.

The Times
www.the-times.co.uk

Current news, breaking news, features, live discussions and forums. Archive going back to at least 2000.

Daily Mail
www.dailymail.co.uk

Current news, breaking news, features and issues, chat, the femail site with 'women's' issues. No archive.

111

Mirror
www.mirror.co.uk

Current news, breaking news, features, archive of recent articles, pictures, front pages for past few months.

Sun
www.thesun.co.uk

News, breaking news, features and pictures. No archive at the time of writing, but is in the process of developing one.

Press Association
www.pa.press.net

This is the web site of the Press Association with a wide range of resources and an extensive archive. This is also the home of the virtual newscaster Ananova (also on *www.ananova.com*). Interesting and useful

The Paperboy
www.thepaperboy.com

A massive resource base of around 5,500 international newspapers. It has a translation facility for subscribers. Subscription is not free, but costs very little per month.

The Onion
www.theonion.com

A satirical online newspaper that manages to be both current and funny.

OTHER RESOURCES

There are a massive number of online resources for people who are researching into newspaper language. This list is not, and is not intended to be, exhaustive, but offers a small number of addresses that provide links to a wider range.

www.mediauk.com

A resource base for communications media. There is a wide range of up-to-date information on newspapers in the UK, including circulation figures and ownership.

www.researchindex.co.uk

Go to the search page and click on 'newspapers'. This will give you links to many of the online regional and national newspapers in the UK.

www.cultsock.ndirect.co.uk

An interesting resource for ideas, essays and concepts about newspapers. The information on this site is updated fairly regularly, but as you will be warned, it doesn't guarantee to be completely up-to-date about rapidly changing issues such as circulation and ownership. Useful links.

index of terms

This is a form of combined glossary and index. Listed below are some of the main key terms used in the book, together with brief definitions for purposes of reference. The page references will normally take you to the first use of the term in the book, where it will be usually shown in **bold**. In some cases, however, understanding of the term can be helped by exploring its uses in more than one place in the book, and accordingly more than one page reference is given.

actional   74
Verbs that refer to processes that can be defined as actions. The actional model can be divided into two kinds – transactive and non-transactive. A transactive verb is a verb in which the action passes from the actor/ agent to the affected. A non-transactive verb is one that refers to an action or process in which there is one entity related to a process. The entity can't easily be classified as actor/agent or affected. For example, in the sentence 'The boy runs', the boy is both performing the action and affected by it. This model is a simplified version of the one given by Hodge and Kress (1979).

active   (see **voice**)

adjunct   (see **adverbial**)

adverbial   31
That part of the clause that carries information about place, manner, time, frequency, degree, cause, etc. It can be an adverb, an adverb phrase, or an adverb clause e.g. 'Madonna gave birth——last night.'.

agent phrase   (see **voice**)

cohesion   99
The pattern of language created within a text, mainly within and across sentence boundaries, and which collectively make up the organisation of larger units of text such as paragraphs. Cohesion can be both lexical and grammatical. Lexical cohesion is established by means of chains of words of related meaning linking across sentences; grammatical cohesion is established by grammatical words – the, this, it, etc.

connotation   18
The associations a word creates.

co-operative principle   107
Proposed by philosopher Paul Grice. Participants in a conversation will co-operate with each other when making their contributions.

deictic   26
Deictic words point out or specify a time, a place, a person, a thing. Deictics can point in various directions, both within the text and outside it.

exophoric   102
Reference outside the text.

grammatical cohesion (see **cohesion**)

grammatical word   19
A word that carries a

115

grammatical rather than a semantic meaning, for example determiners, auxiliary verbs.

graphology 55
The visual aspects of text, including layout and images.

homophones 17
Words that have the same pronunciation but differ in meaning, for example roll, role.

homonym 18
A word that has more than one meaning, meanings that are not closely related, e.g. Lighter = less heavy, lighter = a device for lighting cigarettes.

implicature 107
Meanings that are dependant on the context of the utterance and the text, and share knowledge that may be assumed to exist between narrator and narratee.

intertextuality 18
The way in which a text echoes or refers to another text, e.g. the phrase 'the bloom with a phew' refers to the title of E.M. Forster's novel *A Room with a View*.

lexical cohesion (see **cohesion**)

lexical word 19
A word that carries full semantic meaning.

modality 91
The way in which a text can express an attitude towards a situation, usually through the use of modal verbs (see **modal verb**) and adverbs such as 'probably', 'certainly' or constructions such as 'it is certain that . . .'.

modal verb 91
A verb used to express modality, for example 'must', 'can', 'could', 'will', 'would', 'shall', 'may'.

modifier 21
Premodifier, post-modifier (see **noun phrase**).

non-transactive 75
An actional structure in which there is only one actor or entity and there is no easily identified actor or affected, e.g. 'The boy runs', 'John played tennis'. (see **actional**)

noun phrase 21
A word or group of words with a noun as its head (essential word), with added information or detail in the form of modifiers. Premodifiers come before the head, post-modifiers follow it. Noun phrases have the possible structure of 'determiner', 'premodifier', 'headword' (noun or pronoun), 'post-modifier'. For example, 'he'; 'the strange boy'; 'the strange boy in blue shoes'; are all noun phrases.

passive (see **voice**)

phonological 18
Relating to the sound system of the language. Some phonological devices texts can use are alliteration – the repetition of an initial sound – and phoneme substitution – the replacement of an expected sound by an unexpected one ('hit and myth', rather than 'hit and miss').

phrasal verb 20
A verb followed by a particle (usually a preposition) that together have a specific and independent meaning.

polyseme 18
A word that has two or more closely related meanings, for example 'head' can mean 'part of the body', 'person in charge', 'front of the line', etc.

pragmatics 105

The factors that govern the choice of language in social interaction, and the effects those choices have.

presupposition 106

Inferences or assumptions that are 'built in' to an utterance or text. For example, the utterance "Have you found your dog?" presupposes 1) that the person addressed owns a dog; 2) that the dog was lost.

relational 75

Verbs that involve the relationship between two entities or between an entity and a quality.

semantic field 99

A group of words that are related in meaning, normally as a result of being connected with a particular context of use, for example 'storms', 'thunder', 'rain', 'hail' all belong to the semantic field of weather.

syntax 73

The relationship between elements in a clause.

theme 85

The theme of a clause is usually the first main word unit of a sentence.

transactive 75

A structure in which the action passes from the actor to the affected, e.g. 'The boy hit the ball'. (see **actional**)

transitive 75

The relationship between the verb or verb group, the participants in the action, state or process and other elements of the clause.

voice 83

A grammatical feature which indicates whether the subject in a sentence is the agent of an action or is affected by the action. Voice can be either active or passive, for example. 'The girl threw the ball' (active); 'The ball was thrown by the girl' (passive). The passive voice allows the agent phrase, that is the 'by' phrase, to be deleted: 'The ball was thrown'.

index of main texts

further reading

Fowler, Roger (1991) *Language in the News: Discourse and Ideology in the Press*, Routledge, London.

— Hodge, Bob, Kress, Gunther and Trew, Tony (1979) *Language and Control*, Routledge, London.

Hartley, John (1982) *Understanding News*, Routledge, London.

Herman, Edward S. and Chomsky, Noam (1988) *Manufacturing Consent: The Political Economy of the Mass Media*, Random House, New York.

Mills, Sarah (1995) *Feminist Stylistics*, Routledge, London.

Simpson, Paul (1993) *Language, Ideology and Point of View*, Routledge, London.

references

Hodge, Robert and Kress, Gunther (1993) *Language as Ideology*, 2nd edn, Routledge, London.

Labov, William (1997) *Language in the Inner City. Studies in the Black English Vernacular*, Blackwell, Oxford.

Tunstall, Jeremy (1996) *Newspaper Power. The New National Press in Britain*, Clarendon Press, Oxford.